Making Video Dance

Making Video Dance: A step-by-step guide to creating dance for the screen is the first workbook to follow the entire process of video dance production: from having an idea, through to choreographing for the screen, filming and editing, and distribution. In doing so, it explores and analyses the creative, practical, technical and aesthetic issues that arise when making video dance.

The book is written by award-winning director Katrina McPherson, whose passion for the genre combines with her wide experience of choreographing, directing and teaching video dance.

Making Video Dance contains:

* a detailed explanation of the creative process
* practical exercises to illuminate important stages of the process
* interviews with key international video dance practitioners, including Lea Anderson, Elliot Caplan, David Hinton, Liz Aggiss and Billy Cowie
* a production diary of the making of *The Truth*, providing a fascinating, first-hand account of the challenges of creating a large-scale video dance work
* an introduction by Bob Lockyer, co-founder of the influential BBC/ Arts Council England Dance for the Camera series
* helpful tips and a glossary of terms.

Conceived as an invaluable resource and source of inspiration for those whose imagination is captured by this exciting new art form, *Making Video Dance* will appeal to anyone who wants to know about how to create dance for the screen.

Katrina McPherson is one of the first generation of truly hybrid video dance artists. She has wide experience as a dancer and choreographer, as a director of television arts programmes and as a video dance-maker. Her video dance works include *Pace* (1996), *Moment* (2000 – awarded 'Best Screen Choreography' at the IMZ Dance Screen Festival in Monaco), *Sense-8* (2001) and *The Truth* (2003). Katrina co-runs the production company 'Goat' with Simon Fildes. She has taught extensively and is currently Research Fellow at Dundee University in Scotland.

Making Video Dance

A step-by-step guide to creating dance for the screen

Katrina McPherson

Routledge
Taylor & Francis Group

LONDON AND NEW YORK

First published 2006
by Routledge
2 Park Square, Milton Park, Abingdon, Oxon OX14 4RN

Simultaneously published in the USA and Canada
by Routledge
270 Madison Avenue, New York, NY 10016

Routledge is an imprint of the Taylor & Francis Group, an informa business

The author acknowledges support from the Scottish Arts Council towards the writing of this title.

LOTTERY FUNDED

Designed and typeset in Univers and Avant Garde
by Keystroke, Jacaranda Lodge, Wolverhampton
Printed and bound in Great Britain
by TJ International Ltd, Padstow, Cornwall

British Library Cataloguing in Publication Data
A catalogue record for this book is available from the British Library

Library of Congress Cataloging in Publication Data
McPherson, Katrina.
Making video dance: a step by step guide to creating dance for the screen / Katrina McPherson.
p. cm.
Includes bibliographical references and index.
1. Dance in motion, pictures, television, etc.–Production and direction–Handbooks, manuals, etc. 2. Video recordings–Production and direction–Handbook, manuals, etc. I. Title.
GV1779.M37 2006
791.43'657–dc22
2005030668

ISBN10: 0–415–37942–3 (hbk)
ISBN10: 0–415–37950–4 (pbk)

ISBN13: 9–78–0–415–37942–7 (hbk)
ISBN13: 9–78–0–415–37950–2 (pbk)

For my daughters, Eilidh and Isabella

Contents

Illustrations

All illustrations by Cavan Convery. Photographs of the production of *The Truth* © Simon Fildes.

How did we get here?

Some thoughts on making dance for television

Nearly all my working life, now over forty years, has been involved with television – thirty-five of those have included dance in all its forms. I started work when there were only two television channels in Britain and they broadcast in black and white. In the intervening time, I've seen many technical changes, but the rules for making dance for the screen have remained the same. So it was a pleasure to be asked to contribute to this much-needed book, a step-by-step guide to making video dance.

I first met Katrina at the Banff Centre for the Arts in Canada in 1992, when she was taking part in a Dance and the Camera workshop I was running with Peter Boneham, of Le Groupe de la Place Royale, who was looking after the dance side of the project. They were three exciting weeks which helped a lot of choreographers and video-makers discover some of the wonders of dance for the camera and helped set Katrina off on a very successful career teaching and making dance films. In this chapter I'll look at some of the technical changes that have taken place over those years. I'll ask a few questions; discuss working methods; include a few anecdotes.

The revolution in making dance for the screen that has happened in the past ten or so years would not have been possible without the arrival of the digital chip and with it the lightweight portable video camera, with a built-in recording facility.

In my early days in television, every camera needed two or three 'minders'. They were the engineers, each with a top pocket full of screwdrivers, who nursed these new strange beasts through the working day.

Each of the cameras – and there were only three or four in the studio at once – was attached to a length of cable. This was plugged into the studio wall and took the pictures on their journey, via vision control where they balanced the pictures, to the production gallery, the vision-mixing panel and then to the transmitters and out – through the skies – to the black and white television receiver in your home. I must not forget the sound (we always seem to fall into the danger of doing that and you do it at your peril): the microphones were also attached to the wall and so to the sound-mixing desk. There were no radio mics yet, the extra sound effects were spun in off disc and the music was relayed back into the studio from a quarter-inch tape (no digital recording, or sixteen-track players either).

The cameras, I seem to remember, were full of things called valves and cathode-ray tubes that all had to be 'tuned' to give you a good picture. It took the team of studio engineers an hour and a half to line up all the cameras, as they all were pointed at the black and white Test Card. At the end of that, all you could do was hope that they would work and that they were all balanced to match each other.

A large percentage of the programmes in those days were live, and camera breakdowns, even after all that tender, loving care, were sadly quite common. To cover these little interruptions, or when programmes were shorter than they should have been, there was a collection of 'interval films' that were shown. The most famous of these (in the UK), was the potter's wheel. Shot on film, it showed a potter making something on his wheel. All you saw were his hands and the clay as he worked, always pushing it down to start again, so you never saw the finished thing. (I wonder if Jonathan Burrows could have seen the potter's wheel when he came to make his film *Hands* for the BBC/Arts Council of Great Britain's Dance for the Camera series in 1995.) But the digital revolution has changed all that. To balance your cameras now all you do is press the white balance button. The teams of engineers have gone the way of the interval films. Now, in this multi-channel age, every programme has to run to time and in unified lengths.

Television programmes also have to earn, by whom I've never learnt, their place in a network's schedule and to increase, or at least hold onto, the share of the audience, if you want a re-commission. This is the world of television into which dance programmes now have to fit.

But, in the 1930s, at the very start of public television in the UK, dance had an important role to play, whether it was a group of dancers supporting the star in a light entertainment show or a choreographer making a dance piece for the camera. (Anthony Tudor was, if not in name, almost BBC Television's resident choreographer). In those early days, and right up to the 1960s, there was no way to record the electronic signal that made up the picture electronically. Television programmes were live, i.e. they were happening in the studio at the same time as you watched at home. The time the production team had in the studio was limited, often just one day, and rehearsals were followed immediately by the live transmission. Those rehearsals were really for the cameras, not the performers. They came to the studio word-perfect or, in case of dance, step-perfect.

When the red light went out at the end of the transmission, the job was done and it was on to the next project. If the broadcaster wanted to repeat the programme, the set, dancers and technical crew had to come back into the studio and do the whole thing again. Soon, a simple form of black and white recording was invented: a film camera was pointed at a monitor and the image was filmed, as was broadcast. It got quite sophisticated, but there was no slow motion or instant replay. However, you did have a record of a performance and, luckily, the BBC's video library still contains some wonderful and memorable dance performances recorded in this way.

This was the world of television I joined, and I got involved in dance as a result of being allocated to work with Margaret Dale, the producer/ director who was responsible for nearly all the ballet programmes on BBC Television in the 1960s.

One of the programmes I first worked on with Maggie was *Zodiac*. This was a monthly, dance-based series inspired by that month's star sign. Each of the programmes included a twenty-minute dance story, made especially for television. Among the choreographers who worked on the show were Peter Darrell, who went on to found Scottish Ballet; Norman Morrice, Director of both Ballet Rambert and the Royal Ballet; Kenneth MacMillan and Birgit Culberg, who came over from Sweden to recreate her TV ballet *Adam and Eve*. We made six programmes before we were taken off the air. Why? Because it was impossible, at that time in the UK, to find enough choreographic talent to devise the short ballets that were to have made up the rest of the series.

Zodiac did give me the chance to write the storylines for a couple of dance shorts. I suppose they could be called some of the very first Dance for the Camera projects that I worked on. One was shot in an empty Royal Albert Hall, as a boy and girl search for each other. It ended with a kiss as they met in the empty arena. The final shot looked down from the top of the dome, high above them, as they came together in the arena far below. The other was filmed on the last Circle Line tube train of the night and ended with a sword fight filmed on the train and in and around Westminster Station, but I can't remember why. Both these were shot on 16 mm film, because to record even a short item on video in those days required a full outside-broadcast unit – a television control room in one lorry and another for all the cameras and cables.

Over the years, the electronics used in the making of television programmes has changed enormously. But the thought processes behind them, for choreographer and director, should not have. It's important to remember that film and video production is a very collaborative process, perhaps even more so than the making of a stage production.

Both need set and costume designers, but for film and television you also need key personnel, such as a lighting cameraperson and an off-line and on-line editor. Listen to what comments they have on your ideas, remember they have a lot of experience, and benefit from it. You also have an upper tier, one that includes the commissioners that bring the money, the producers and the executive producers, who have control of that money. All feel that they have a say in your production. Remember that it is they who must help to make sure you work within budget. They are also the ones who will fight for you, if there are any problems.

Working as I have with Rodney Wilson, my co-executive producer on the Dance for the Camera series, I have the feeling that we both think of those projects as our children. This is because we would read the original ideas, be part of the selection process, have input in pre-production discussions, agree the budget and then, the most difficult role, the first rough-cut viewing.

This viewing is ideally held when there are three or four days left in the cutting room and all the producers come to look at the film they are responsible for. I've been a director myself and have lived through the experience. It can be frightening and daunting, but looking back on a long working life, mostly positive. However, as an executive producer, I've stood outside edit suites, just before pressing the bell to go in, thinking 'Why am I putting myself through this?'. And I also know that, upstairs in the cutting room, the choreographer, director and editor are feeling the same way. Both sides have to remember, though, that we all want the same thing: the best video dance possible.

Directors and choreographers now have a great tool at their disposal: the personal video camera. Use it. Look at the world through your lens, notice the difference a change in lens height can make, watch movement in the frame. And it doesn't have to be dancers in the frame – people walking in the street will do just as well. But remember, what you put in the frame and then record is all you have to work with during the edit.

If you want to try making a dance for the camera today, then you are lucky. Advances in video and sound mean that you can make work without the vast infrastructure that I had to have when I started. The digital revolution has made it possible, if you want, for you to become choreographer, director, cameraperson and editor all in one, a one-person band in fact. Enjoy it. I wish I were starting now.

The past forty years have been exhilarating, I've worked on some wonderful projects with some very challenging people, and some exciting films and videos have resulted. I hope you find this book useful, as it guides you through the process with its tips and comments from the experts. Do try the exercises; things often make more sense when you actually do them! I hope you have as much fun as I've had working with dance and the camera for all these years, and it's not over yet.

Bob Lockyer

Notes on using the exercises

A series of exercises are included in the book, designed to accompany key stages of the process. These are intended to enhance understanding of the topics covered. Depending on their subject, some of these are written exercises and others are practical. As well as moving bodies, the latter require access to some digital video equipment, including a camera and tripod and, in later chapters, an edit system loaded with a basic editing software such as iMovie. In the practical exercises, it may be useful to have some short sequences of choreographed movement ready to be performed by the dancers. If your background is not in dance, then this may require collaboration with a choreographer or dancer who can devise movement.

Acknowledgements

My thanks first to the Scottish Arts Council's Creative Scotland Award panel for enabling me to research and write this book.

Thanks also to Talia Rodgers at Routledge for her faith in the project, to Minh Ha Duong for her advice and assistance, and to the readers who gave me very helpful guidance in the writing of the text, in particular Martha Curtis of the Virginia Commonwealth University in the USA.

Many thanks are due to all the contributors whom I interviewed for the book. Our conversations not only provided useful quotes, but also helped to clarify for me many of the topics discussed in the book. I am particularly grateful to Bob Lockyer, whose enthusiasm and input into the project has been immeasurable.

I also want to acknowledge the many dancers, choreographers and other creative people with whom I have collaborated over the years and the numerous students on workshops and courses that I have taught, all who have contributed to the development of my approach to making video dance and therefore to this book.

My love and appreciation goes to my patient and ever-supportive family. Finally, the biggest thanks of all goes to my life partner and long-term collaborator Simon Fildes, without whom nothing would happen.

Introduction

I wrote this book because I could not find one like it. I was teaching courses on video dance and looking for a book about the processes of making video dance to recommend to students. Whilst there are many texts on film- and video-making in general, I found none focusing on the specific and unique concerns and possibilities that arise when you make dance specifically for the screen.

Video dance is currently in the middle of an explosion of popularity, spurred on by the ever-increasing availability and flexibility of digital-video technology. This enables artists to create work with a 'just do it' spirit. So, in a similar mood, I decided that the best way to solve my problem was to write the book myself! The opportunity arose when I made a successful application to the Scottish Arts Council for a Creative Scotland Award, with which I proposed to research and write a workbook for making video dance.

My own impulse to make dance for the screen came when, on graduating from the Laban Centre, London in 1988 with a degree in Dance Theatre, I wanted to bring dance to as wide an audience as possible. Although I was keen to be a choreographer, I was reluctant to make work that, I felt then, would only be seen by other dance enthusiasts at one of the small, dedicated dance theatres in the big cities.

Around that time, in the UK, new ways of making dance for television were being explored through ground-breaking schemes such as Channel

4's Dancelines and the BBC's Dance House. These offered a refreshing alternative to the broadcasts of full-length ballets 'live' from the stage at Covent Garden Opera House that then made up the majority of dance on UK television. Now experienced film and television directors and choreographers were being brought together to experiment with movement, cameras and editing, and the results were broadcast to audiences that, although perhaps small by prime-time television standards, were inconceivable in a live theatre context. As a young dance-maker, I saw many of these short 'video dance' works and was inspired and excited by the potential I could see in this new, hybrid medium.

Fifteen-plus years later, video dance has emerged as an art form in its own right, and there are now many opportunities beyond television for this kind of work to be funded and seen. In fact, there are arguably many more opportunities to make work *not* for broadcast than there are *for* broadcast. The money to make the majority of my own video dance has come from both public and private commissions, and the resulting works have been screened all over the world: at festivals and in cinemas, theatres and galleries.

Making Video Dance is based on my own experiences as a video dance-maker and as a director of arts programmes for television, working primarily in the UK. The structure of the book follows the creative process of making dance for the screen and takes inspiration from dance-making as well as film- and television-production practices. Whatever the context in which you are making video dance, and whether it is intended for broadcast or not, I believe that the process described provides a useful model on which to base your creative journey.

Similarly, whilst my own work has been made almost exclusively within the tradition of Western theatre dance, I believe that most, if not all, of the artistic, aesthetic and practical concerns explored in this book are applicable to different types, traditions and definitions of dance.

What I have tried to do with this book is to answer some of questions that arose for me as a dance person moving into the world of video production with the intention of making dance for the screen. The perspective taken is of the director, for it is he or she who needs to have the complete overview of every aesthetic and practical aspect of the production. I trust that what is contained in the book will be as useful for the choreographer-turned-director as it will be to the film- or video-maker coming new to dance for the screen. Similarly, it can also offer insight and guidance to the choreographer, dancer, composer, producer and any other creative individual who finds themselves involved in making video dance.

In many respects, I have aimed high with what is included in the text. If this is your first experience of making video dance, say on an undergraduate college course, then some of the information – for example, on budgeting and cost reports, or the involvement of production or costume designers – may not feel so relevant to your situation. However, I wanted to find a balance between staying true to the process as I know it and providing useful information and advice for many different people, whatever their experiences and needs. So, in order to make the text as accessible as possible, it has been divided into clearly marked sections and is carefully indexed. Whilst holding onto my wish to follow the structure of the video dance production process, I have used the first chapters to explore the basics – having an idea, looking down the lens – before allowing the information to become more detailed and advanced as the process evolves. There is also a glossary of terms often used in the video dance-making process at the end of the book.

It is beyond the scope of the book, however, to go into great detail about some of the more technical aspects of video production. This information also tends to go quickly out of date. And so, when required, my suggestion is that you seek out specialist manuals or textbooks on video technology or do some research on the Internet. The book also has a related web site – www.makingvideodance.com – which I invite you to take a look at. It has information on where to see work, detailed videographies of the contributors, as well as updates on and additions to various topics covered in the book and links to related web sites.

In his preface to this book, Bob Lockyer puts current digital video dance-making practice into a historical context. Bob's contribution to the development of video dance has been enormous. For over thirty years, from his position as Producer of Dance at the BBC in London, he fought long and hard to raise the profile of dance on television and to create new possibilities for work to be made.

Also included in the book are quotes from specially conducted interviews with key video dance practitioners from the UK, USA, Canada and

Australia. My choice of who to interview was based on having heard these individual artists speak about their own creative, aesthetic and practical experiences of video dance. I found them all to be immensely inspiring and thought-provoking and I am sure that you will feel the same.

A word now about definitions. Throughout this book, I have chosen to use the term 'video dance', as oppose to 'dance film' or 'screen dance', which are two of the various other terms that are often used to describe this genre. By doing this, I am acknowledging the fact that the vast majority of people making this kind of work are now doing so using digital video technology at some, if not all, of the production stages.

However, the term 'video dance' does not exclude work that has been shot, or even edited, using a film format. It is rather a catch-all term to describe this relatively new art form that fuses avant-garde approaches to dance-making with innovation in video art, film and television-making practices.

Some of the other practitioners who are featured in the book use different terms, such as 'dance film' or 'screen dance', to describe their work. Within the context of the quotes that appear in the book, they are referring to what I would call 'video dance'. To add to this mix, we all use the term 'filming' to describe the process of capturing images and sound in camera, even if the format being used is video.

The challenge to anyone making video dance is to invent a new language for the screen. What we are creating is not a dance, nor is it a video of a dance, or even for that matter simply a video. Our ambition must be to find and communicate ideas that can only be expressed through this art form that combines the media of dance and video, using a style and syntax that is unique to video dance. This is as challenging for the creators as it is for the viewers.

Making video dance is difficult, and one of the traps that people often fall into is that they shy away from using choreographed dance movement in their work. Our agenda – as video dance-makers – must be to put dance movement – rich, textured, complex, rhythmical, compelling dance movement – at the centre of our work, as it is this that communicates. The worst scenario, which must be avoided, is that the movement, or dance, content of the work seems like an afterthought; the last thing to be considered after location, design, camera and editing style.

There is another danger: because video dance is screen-based work – and therefore by default associated with television – the expectation is often that everything should be immediately obvious on one viewing and that there is a sense of narrative closure. Video dance offers much greater potential than that: it can create fresh and compelling visual and aural experiences; it can challenge perceptions; it can illuminate concepts; it can stimulate emotion; it can be funny, sad, disturbing, beautiful.

If video dance is to matter, then we must strive to make a work that on one level demands analysis and thought, but on the other is enjoyed and appreciated, whether that be on a storytelling, action-packed, impressionistic or experiential level.

Katrina McPherson

C O N T E N T S

First Steps

As we will see over the course of this book, the process of making video dance involves the weaving together of various aesthetic and practical elements and the input of many of people. It can be a long, complex and un-predictable creative journey, one that can be made a lot easier with a clear idea to guide you.

Expressed intention

We make work to be experienced by others.

Our work needs to draw people in and take them on a journey.

It must intrigue, fascinate, entertain, inspire, challenge, provoke and move. Above all, it must communicate. What it communicates is your decision.

You might want to tell a particular story or to present the life of a character or group of characters. You might want to create a certain mood or quality. You might want to break new ground in terms of the art form.

It is possible – in fact, it is likely – that you might want to do all of the above and more.

When you start to make a new piece of work, you may not know exactly what the finished work will look or sound like, nor how long it will be, nor its shape or structure. But what is vital is that you are clear of your intention.

Your intention is the core idea of your work, the concept that holds everything together. Being clear in your intention will help you to maximise the options and negotiate the obstacles that confront you as you make your work. It will help you to decide what is right and what is wrong for your video dance.

However, the wonderful thing about making art is that, no matter how clear your intention or specific your ideas, once the work goes out into the world, you cannot control how it is understood by those who experience it. The viewer's own life experiences will determine what he or she takes from the work.

Your role as an artist is to offer up something that merits the attention of other human beings and which, to the best your ability, does so with originality, honesty and clarity.

'You go out into the world and you try to realise an idea. You struggle with it, you wrestle with it, you try things – it works, or it doesn't work. You try again. That's what I think everyone's work should be about.'

Elliot Caplan, director

Different starting points

Every video dance needs to have an idea to start it off.

It might be a story or a dramatic situation. It might be another work of art – for example, the paintings of a particular artist or era, a film or a piece of music. It might also be a movement idea, a camera or editing technique, or a specific location that offers up an idea.

Some of the most usual starting points for video dance are:

- themes
- stories
- formal
- visual
- aural.

'There are central ideas or motifs that come up again and again in my work. One of them is flight and winged creatures, and that image appears and reappears in almost every single piece that I've ever done. To the point that I start to think: "I must stop having winged creatures in my work!" '

Litza Bixler, director/choreographer

Themes

The theme of a work is a single idea to which all aspects of the work relate.

Choosing a theme as the starting point for your work helps you to be clear about the essence of the work, whilst at the same time enabling your imagination and creativity to expand and elaborate.

Themes can be:

- emotional – for example, loss or joy
- experiential – for example, speed, transformation, flight
- symbolic – for example, one against many, the search for love
- physical – for example, water, earth, gravity
- action-based – for example, climbing, running, falling, swooping.

A theme can be tackled in very different ways.

For example, the theme 'Transformation' could be represented by:

- a story in which frog changes into a prince
- editing, in which one type of material – for example, a woman performing solo shot in close-up – is gradually replaced by another, perhaps a wide shot of the same dancer, dressed in different costume, dancing a duet with another dancer.

An emotional theme, such as 'Joy', could be developed through the idea of weightlessness, which involves the exploration of gravity as represented by video dance footage that has been filmed entirely with the camera upside down.

In a theme-based video dance, all aspects of the process, including choreographing the dancers' movement, design, filming and editing are developed to represent the theme.

Themes can be culturally specific, which means that, whilst they may be understood pretty much as you intended by others who share your experience of the world, they may be read very differently in another context.

'A common theme for us is definitely about exploring the human form in the landscape. Most of our films have been about solo characters and their relationship to the environment.'

Rosemary Lee, choreographer/director

Stories

A story describes a sequence of events.

Most often, stories are about characters in specific situations and their interaction and developing relationships with other characters.

Video dance works often take stories as their starting point. There are a few reasons for this:

- People like stories. We tell and listen to stories all the time: in the news and the newspapers, in books, in the cinema and on television. We even recount the fragmented images of our dreams in story form over the breakfast table.
- Traditionally, film and television have been used as the vehicle for telling stories and, as a result, we feel comfortable when we recognise a familiar approach to the medium, even if the dialogue that we might usually expect is absent.
- It is often very much easier to describe a story than any other type of idea and, as we will see later in this chapter, how successfully you can communicate the idea for your work to other people, such as possible funders or collaborators, is crucial in getting your video dance made.

The stories you choose to base your work on can be:

- taken from the world around you
- inspired by fairy tales or fables
- based on historical lives and events
- drawn from your own experiences
- those that flow from your imagination.

In most feature and short films, stories have a clear sense of beginning, middle and end, although not necessarily presented in that order.

In video dance, the structure is often less obvious, or at least the resolution of the story is not necessarily that clear, and the work is (often) intentionally ambiguous.

'Because we knew that *Heartbeat* was going to be shown on TV, we deliberately decided to have a clear sense of narrative. We actually sat down and decided that. Not all of our work is like that. We've made other things which were much more surreal and abstract, about interesting, unusual, bizarre movement for its own sake, which I also think is a great approach. But we just felt that for this context, we didn't want to alienate people; rather, we wanted to draw them in.'

Litza Bixler, director/choreographer

Formal ideas

Formal ideas are inspired by the technical and creative possibilities of the medium. The starting point is not an external subject, but rather the medium itself. How it is used becomes the subject of the work.

Formal ideas can often be kicked off by questions. For example:

- What happens if the camera is always in motion?
- How do we represent speed on screen?

Formal ideas can also be based on restrictions on, for example, how the dancers move, how the camera is used, how the material will be edited or a combination of all three. You might:

- set off to explore what happens if you only ever see a particular body part in the frame – for example, faces, hands or feet
- set a rule that your video dance will last the length of one continuous zoom in and create the dancers' choreography around that shot
- plan to explore the effect of looping and repetition in the edit, where sequences are created by dropping and replacing shots, according to preconceived mathematical patterns.

'When I did *Touched*, the formal idea was: "Let's try and make a dance film entirely in close-up." With *Birds*, the idea I started with was: "Let's try and make a dance film where all the choreography is created through editing." I arrived at these formal ideas through making dance films. When you work on each film it makes you think more about this whole relationship between dance and film.'

David Hinton, director

Visual

It may be that the first ideas for your video dance are inspired by a particular visual image. This may be:

- a particular location, such as a beach, or a flight of stairs
- a specific object, such as a piece of furniture, or a car
- a piece of clothing, such as a pair of gloves or a dress.

It can even be an interest in exploring the quality of particular colours and texture, as created through movement on the screen.

As we will explore in later chapters, the development of all video dance involves considering design, location and costume, but for some artists, these elements are the starting point of their work and everything else (choreography, camera, editing and sound) stems from there.

Aural

The first images you have for a new work might be aural rather than visual. As the soundtrack of your video dance has equal impact to the pictures, beginning with what will be heard is a very effective method.

- An existing piece of music can be used as inspiration, with the story, emotion or structure of the music providing the starting point for your video dance.
- Music can also be used illustratively in that you create images that represent your interpretation of the tones and qualities of the music.
- You may have a more formal or conceptual idea based on, for example, certain types of sound or the relationship between sounds and images.

Even if your idea is not a directly aural one, from very early on in the process you must think about how you will use sound in your video dance.

The soundtrack – that is, the design of everything that is heard in your video dance and how it relates to the visuals – is crucial to how your work will be experienced by others, and it will be something that you will be asked about from the start, by potential collaborators and by anyone who you might be approaching to fund your work.

'I started from a piece of music, Schubert's "Death and the Maiden", and broke it down and tried to write it in my own words. I tried to describe the qualities of the music and what the music was telling me. I just closed my eyes and listened to the music over and over again and I wrote a story, a fairy tale about the day Death meets the Maiden in the forest.'

Laura Taler, choreographer/director

Multi-layered works

Very often, the starting point for your video dance will be a combination of a variety of types of ideas, formulated into a coherent, multi-layered concept.

In my own video dance work, I often set out with a formal question. For example, What happens when a particular relationship between dancer and camera or an approach to editing or the use of sound is followed through? However, my work is never purely formal; rather I use these ideas as a vehicle to express aspects of human existence as I perceive it.

Where ideas come from

There are times when almost all of us are in the position of having to think up an idea for a new work.

It may be that you are intrigued by video dance as an art form but have not yet found the right idea to start off with. Or maybe you are a collaborative team that wants to make some work together, but do not yet have a theme.

Or perhaps you are in a situation in which you are committed to making a video dance – for example, on a course or workshop – or you want to apply to a particular video dance funding scheme that has come up, and you need to find an idea that fits.

It might be that your mind is brimming with ideas for video dance works, in which case you won't need any tips on how to generate new ones. On the other hand, if at times your mind feels blank when trying to come up with something fresh, the following suggestions may be helpful.

- Think about the issues that concern you, thoughts that affect you emotionally and the stories that intrigue you. Work out how you can explore these ideas in video dance.
- Look around and take inspiration from the behaviour and actions of the people you see and interact with, or from animals, or the environment.

- Go out with a camera and look at things through the lens. Ideas will come.
- Be inspired by other works of art, by books, films, poems, architecture, music and dance.

Ask yourself some questions.

- What do you want to communicate?
- Are you interested in passing on a specific message or in telling a story, making people laugh, or feel good or sad?
- Do you want to create beauty, or to focus on the difficult and dark areas of life?
- Do you want to combine different ideas, thoughts and feelings in your work?

It is important to remember that each person has a unique way of looking at the world. Your experience of life is different from the experiences of other people, and you have your own perception of and feelings about the world around you.

As an artist, you need to discover how that personal vision can be expressed through the creative possibilities offered by your chosen art form.

'My advice would be to try and watch as much of what is out there as possible. What you really need to do to ensure success is to come up with a strong idea. You have to know what will make your dance film stand out in the marketplace and you can't do that unless you know what is out there.'

Erin Brannigan, curator

Developing your idea

No matter how intangible your idea is to start with, the very act of making art involves a continued process of clarification. What starts off as a vague notion will become more and more specific as your thoughts become a reality and as decisions are made that define the work.

Some people begin with a very clear idea of what it is that they plan to create. Others work in a more exploratory way, following a process and shaping the work as they go.

However, you will inevitably find that as soon as you start to take your idea for a video dance beyond the initial flash of inspiration, you will be faced with a number of questions. These are the kinds of questions that once you involve others in your project you will also invariably be asked. They include:

- Who are these people on screen?
- What are they doing?
- Why are they doing it?
- Where are they?
- What are they wearing?

These may seem like very literal questions if, for example, your intention is to explore a formal idea. However, it is impossible to avoid addressing them because video dance has, in almost every case, the actions of human beings at its core, and for that reason, even the most 'abstract' work will raise these issues.

Similarly, they may seem like very specific questions to be asking so soon in the creative process, but the answers will reveal the essence of your work and are important to clarify early on, as they help you to make decisions about everything, from location and costume to camera work and editing. Knowing what you are setting out to achieve will help you enormously to steer a course through the process of making video dance.

Because video dance production involves different layers of creativity and many practical and logistical considerations, you will often find yourself having to make decisions about aspects of the production that feel a long way off, and before you feel ready to do so. For example, in order to know how you want to shoot a particular scene, you will need to have an idea about how you plan to edit, and, before you have even created one step of choreography, you can find yourself deciding what the dancers are going to wear, in order that their costumes can be completed in time for the first day of filming.

This is one of the biggest challenges that will face you when making screen-based work. Potentially difficult situations can be made a lot easier if the idea for your video dance is clear and well thought through, and certain questions can be answered early on in the process.

New work or re-work

Not all video dance is conceived from the outset as work for the screen. A video dance can also be based on an already existing live choreography. The process involved is often described as a 'camera re-work'.

In the past, festivals and commissioning bodies have differentiated between video dance that is based on an existing choreography, originally created for live performance and video dance that has been conceived and choreographed for the screen. However, the issue is not so much whether the choreography originally started life on the stage and was then re-worked into a video dance, but rather how that process is carried out.

Unlike documentation, where the aim is to record how the choreography looked on stage, the re-work is an attempt to create a screen version, related to but entirely independent of the existing live work.

The process involves reconceiving the live choreography completely as a video dance. This often means altering the structure of the choreography by dropping and/or adding sections or scenes, losing, adding or changing the music, as well as setting the action in a location.

'I enjoy directing work that has already been on the stage most. There is an existing choreography that somebody has made and, as screen director, you are there to interpret it, which gives you much more freedom than when you are starting from scratch, working with a choreographer.'

Ross MacGibbon, director

There are definite benefits in making a video dance based on an already existing live work.

*   You and your collaborators have something real to look at, discuss and build on. The creative process can be a great deal less complex when there is a clear idea and a body of choreography with which to work.
*   Time will already have been spent on the creation and rehearsal of the choreography. The work may have had many performances in the theatre, which will mean that the dancers will be in tune and

comfortable with the movement. This can be a great advantage over a video dance that has been conceived and created for the screen, when typically budgets and schedules do not allow sufficient time to develop the choreography or for the dancers to become familiar with the material.

- If you are in the situation of needing to raise funds to make your video dance, this can be much easier with a re-work, as there is already something for the people with the money to look at. You can invite them to go and see the work live, or show them documentation and images taken from the performance.

All successful re-works of live choreography have one thing in common: they have been entirely reconceived according to the creative possibilities of the screen. A mistake made in much video dance – and this can be the case whether it is based on an already existing live work or created specially for the screen – is that the approach to space and to time belongs to the stage rather than to the screen.

Reconsidered space

Unlike in the theatre, in video dance there is no 'front' from where the audience will view the work. The camera represents the viewer's eyes and, as we will explore in greater depth in Chapter 2, the camera can move anywhere in relation to the dance.

In a live context, you would normally only see the dance from one point in space at a time – unless you are in a promenade show, where you can walk around the choreography as it is being performed. Even if you see the same choreography over a series of performances and at each one choose to view from a different seat in the theatre, your relationship to the movement will essentially remain the same for the duration of that performance.

In video dance, however, the viewer's perspective on the action can be changed shot by shot and even within one shot, as the camera moves in relation to the choreography. This creates a different, much more active and three-dimensional experience of space, on screen rather than in the theatre.

Reconsidered time

Likewise, the perception of time in video dance is other from that in a live performance.

Most people experience the fact that images viewed on screen are absorbed very quickly. This means, in effect, that time seems to go faster: what might feel like a reasonable duration for an event to develop on stage may feel much too long in a video dance.

In later chapters, when we explore approaches to editing, we will see how it is often what is 'left out' of a sequence that creates both interest and pace. In video dance, you may choose only to show fragments of a phrase of choreography, missing out various moments along the way and thereby creating a time frame unique to the screen. By concentrating time like this, the viewer's imagination comes into play and on-screen energy is created.

The challenge of transformation

One of the dangers of making video dance based on an already existing live work is that there may be a resistance to the extent to which the live choreography must be transformed.

Whoever is calling the shots – whether it is the choreographer-now-turned-director or a director new to the project – must have the ability, the freedom and the bravery to rethink the work completely, according to what works for the screen.

The intention may be to hold on to the essence of the live work, but this must be done without being restricted by any sense of having to be faithful to the stage version.

Collaboration in video dance

'With *boy*, I had the idea of the boy on the beach, and the director Peter Anderson said "I think he's going to play with another person." My response was: "But I don't want anyone else there; I just want it to be him, completely alone in the landscape." And he said, "It's very hard to make a solo for the camera." So he brought in the doppelganger idea. It's very collaborative, but often I'll come up with the initial idea and then Peter will find a way to realise it and enhance it.'

Rosemary Lee, choreographer/director

The fact that video dance brings together two different art forms – video and dance – which themselves incorporate many different creative elements, such as design, lighting and sound – gives it enormous potential as a creative medium. It also means that, in almost every case, the production process will involve various artists and technicians coming together to work towards one goal.

As we saw in the introduction to this book, in the UK at least, the convention has been that a choreographer and a director should collaborate to create dance for the screen. Now, increasingly, we are seeing situations in which choreographers both make the movement and direct, or composers collaborate with dancers, or choreographers and editors produce and direct their own work.

How artists choose to share their vision and responsibilities and to contribute to the creative process varies in each collaboration team and in every project. Common to all, however, remains the need for a clear vision and, as important but sometimes even trickier, an understanding of what is expected of each of the collaborators.

This can be hard, especially if people have not worked together previously, or if one or more have not made work for the screen before. What you read in this book will help you to clarify who needs to do what at different stages in the process.

When choreographers and directors work together, usually the most crucial question is: Who is in control? The answer is not always that straightforward. Choreographers are used to being the person in charge of their own work. Their live production is their vision and they oversee every aspect of it. Similarly, directors are used to having overall control of a film or video project.

To make successful video dance, someone has to maintain the overall vision for the work. Their role must be to steer the project, working with the other collaborators but taking ultimate responsibility for the processes followed and decisions made. It is easier if it is one person who has this 'final say', and it is usually the person who has assumed the director role, whether they are the director or choreographer/director.

Sometimes two (or more) people will insist that they are co-directing. If this is the case, they have to be extra clear on the intention of the work and be able to operate as a watertight unit. There are many challenges in the process of making video dance, and negotiating these successfully becomes impossible if the project has two leaders who are pulling in different directions.

As I have already suggested, collaboration in the video dance-making process is not limited to the roles of choreographer and director. As will become obvious through the course of this book, many elements draw together to create video dance, and some of these require if not specialist experience, then certainly the attention of someone whose sole responsibility is for that particular aspect of the production.

If you are making your first video dance within a college or workshop context, then you will probably find that some of those amongst you are keen to choreograph or direct or both, whereas others may feel inspired to light and shoot, to design, or to create the soundtrack for the work. If you are working within a professional context, then the description of the specific responsibilities held by the various people who may work on the production, as outlined in Chapter 5, will hopefully provide serve as a useful clarification and checklist.

However you choose to work, the final word must be to reiterate the need for a solid intention and clear direction. In subsequent chapters of this book, we will come across many of the ways in which the distinct roles and responsibilities can be brought together at each stage of the process. The most important thing to realise is that, ultimately, all artistic elements must be 'subordinate' to the video dance. This means that decisions being made need to be done so on the basis of what is right for the video dance, as it appears on screen, and for no other reason.

'I think that you have to really understand the different roles and know what is whose responsibility. If you are not clear beforehand, you will end up with compromise – a revolting hybrid. The whole point of having a director is to have one unifying point of view, even when working in a collaborative way. A choreographer usually functions as a director in live work, but this isn't always the

case in filmed work. When there are two or more people in these roles, compromise may occur, unless the roles are thoroughly clarified and any conflicting
responsibilities removed.'

Lea Anderson, choreographer

Finding the words

I am always amazed how much writing is involved in making video dance. Although there are other tools that one can use for visualising the work before it is made, ultimately you will have to at some point – and probably repeatedly – sit down and write up your idea. It is worth finding ways of enjoying this part of the process as, let's face it, most projects never get past this stage.

Writing down your ideas is an excellent way of capturing the thoughts and images that are whizzing around your head. And there is nothing like sitting down with a piece of paper in front of you to make those ideas disappear from view. But you must persevere – I find that it is in the struggling to find the words to describe vague images or concepts that they clarify into a tangible idea.

In the early stages, it may be that you are writing only for yourself, in order to work out your ideas. You may come to the conclusion that there is not really enough to go on at the moment and that you need to do more thinking and research in order to develop the idea further.

If you are developing ideas with someone else, writing your ideas down is often an essential part of the collaborative process. It forces you to express your thoughts, to describe images and to shape your shared vision.

Another important reason for writing down your ideas is that, if you want to raise money to make your work, this will invariably require some kind of written description. The extent and format of what is required will vary, but you can be sure that you will need to write a page or so of text, outlining the film you want to make. This text is usually referred to as a 'treatment'.

A well-written treatment will not only serve the purpose of helping to raise funds for your film, it will also help to introduce your project to potential collaborators. It is a very useful way for them to understand your intentions. People often refer to the idea of 'singing from the same hymn sheet'. Your treatment will serve as your 'hymn sheet'. It makes sense to spend time and energy on writing it.

'I like the difficulty of having to describe what I do, because it forces me to think about ideas and find some words that describe what I'm doing. But if I'm not successful, then I have to go back to it again and find a better way to describe it. I'm a little put off by the process. I wish it were easier, because it takes too much time and that's what I resent. But there isn't another way. It is incumbent on us as practitioners to have a language to describe what we do.'

Elliot Caplan, director

Writing a treatment

A treatment is not a shot-by-shot outline, but rather it should provide a clear sense of the essence of the film: what it is about; what it will look and sound like; its atmosphere, tone and quality.

There are no formulae for writing treatments, but there are certain things that are useful to think about that can help you find an effective style and approach.

- When writing your treatment, bear in mind the audience, both of the finished work and of the written document itself.
- Do your research. If you are making reference to real events or particular ideas, then do so accurately.
- Be original in your ideas.
- Be honest about what it is you want to do and do not be afraid to pursue your own line of exploration, even if it feels different from what seems to be popular at the time. If your idea is well thought through (and again, this is where the writing process can help) and clearly presented, you have a good chance of being able to convince people of your idea's worth and viability.
- Be intelligent about how you write down and present the idea, but also do not frighten people off by being too clever or obscure.
- Be succinct. (Guidelines will often limit word count.)

Tip!

I always avoid direct references to work by other artists in a treatment, as I feel that this will inevitably bring with it resonances for the reader that might not be your intention.

- Try to find the right style of writing for your video dance. You can convey so much through your choice of words, writing style and even the way the page is laid out.
- Your treatment may well address the questions described earlier in this chapter: Who are these people on screen? What are they doing? Why are they doing it? Where are they? What are they wearing?
- Your treatment should describe the approach you plan to take to the soundtrack of your work.
- Name the core collaborators on the project: director, choreographer and composer, and, along with the treatment, supply details of their previous experience in the form of curriculum vitae or biographies.
- You might also want to consider naming any other key personnel, for example, the cameraperson or editor that you plan to work with. Don't make this up though – if you say someone is going to be working on the project, they should have, at least in principle, agreed to do so.
- Ask someone else to read a draft of your treatment. Find out what questions they are left with after reading it, and find a succinct way of answering these questions within your treatment.

'I'm a bit too poetic – I've always got three describing words for everything. I tend to do a little summary in italics at the top. Then I might explain how it's going to be shot and edited and the overall style. It's quite detailed really, as we know the sort of landscape and the nature of relationship between the character and their environment that we want to work with.'

Rosemary Lee, choreographer/director

Treatment checklist

Your treatment should include:

1. A concise expression of the core idea of your video dance
2. A description of the look and atmosphere of the work
3. An idea of the structure of the video dance
4. The proposed length of the work
5. A description of the soundtrack
6. Names of collaborators and key personnel with whom you plan to work on the project.

'With *Motion Control* I wrote the treatment like a piece of poetry. The opening reads as follows: "The camera wrenches itself from underneath the ground and travels vertically up for 10 feet in a micro-second. Intense green. Vivid blue. Behaving like a meercat. The surrounding landscape is observed with irregular staccato shifts. The camera whiffs an odour and is off." So you see, the camera is directed within the treatment. I wrote it like I saw it. I wrote from the camera's point of view and it had an intense physicality.'

Liz Aggiss, choreographer/director

Exercises

The following exercises are designed to suit the needs of either a workshop group, or an individual working alone, and neither require access to equipment or dancers.

Types of ideas

Take five minutes to come up with an idea based on one of the five categories listed below.

1. Theme
2. Story
3. Formal
4. Visual
5. Aural

If you are in a class or workshop, work in pairs. Brainstorm and then describe the idea to the rest of the group.

Alternatively, write up the idea as briefly yet as fully as possible.

Now discuss, or consider, how the idea relates to its starting point, how it represents a category and what other types of idea it may contain or could be developed to include as another layer.

Work of art

Take ten minutes, either in pairs or alone, to develop an idea for a video dance based on another work of art. Your starting point can be a painting, photo, piece of music, poem and so on, and it is up to you how you interpret it from a thematic, story, formal, visual or aural point of view.

Either describe your idea to the rest of the group, or write it up in a paragraph or two.

Writing a treatment

Write a 200–400-word treatment based one of the following three phrases.

1. 'A twisted shoulder; a head thrown back; a look to the side.'
2. 'If my footsteps follow yours, do we make a path?'
3. 'A space of Time.'

'What's really funny is that I leave the proposal at a certain point and I think "Of course I'm just going to do whatever I want." And I make the film and it leads me off in all sorts of directions. But then I go back to the proposal and I read it, and I think, "Oh, I've made exactly what I wrote." It's not always that way, but I would say 90 per cent of the time it is.'

Laura Taler, choreographer/director

CONTENTS

CHAPTER 2

Dance and the Camera

Experiencing how the lens works in relation to movement is fundamental to understanding how to approach making dance for the screen. This next chapter explores the role of the camera in video dance.

The camera's role

The camera is a lead performer in your video dance.

It is the eye through which the viewer sees.

It is a key collaborator in your work.

The camera frames the world of your video dance. It can create mood and capture atmosphere. It can convey emotion, tell a story, represent a perspective and be part of the action.

Through the use of different shots and angles, the camera can take the viewer to places they could not usually reach. The lens can enter the dancer's kinesphere – the personal space around them that moves with them as they dance – focusing on a detail of movement and allowing an intimacy that would be unattainable in a live performance context.

How the camera moves in relation to the performers is also an important aspect of filming dance. As the choreographed camera – whether handheld or on a track or a jib – moves through space, it alters the viewer's perception of the dance, rendering it three-dimensional and creating a fluid and lively viewing experience.

Framing dance

'You have a rectangle, whether it's a screen or a canvas or a stage, and then what do you do with it? That's the starting point. There are infinite ways to fill that rectangle in interesting ways and that's what art is to me.'

Elliot Caplan, director

The frame is very important because it represents the screen on which the viewer will watch your work.

The frame is the rectangle created by the camera lens.

The frame always has this rectangle shape, although the exact ratio of the length of the sides and the length of the top and bottom of the rectangle can be different. (You can also change the shape of the frame by masking off areas, but the image will still be viewed on a rectangular screen.)

The subject of the frame does not have to be placed in the middle; the rectangle can be filled in many different ways, and the composition of the frame will encourage the viewer to see things in a certain way.

Framing that frustrates the audience's view of the 'whole', by showing only a small fragment of, for example, the body in motion, forces the viewer's imagination to come into play.

It is often what is excluded from the frame, rather than what is included in the frame, that will create interest and energy in the design of a shot.

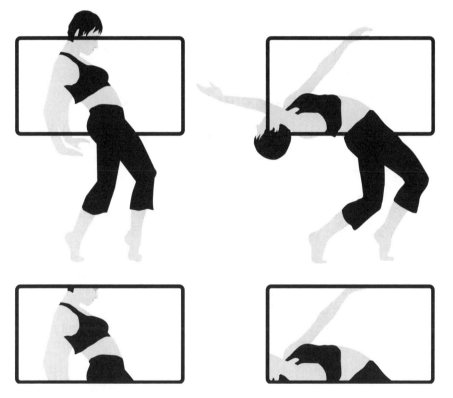

Figure 2.1 **Framing that frustrates the audience's view**

The kind of questions that you will ask yourself when you are looking at a frame might include:

- To where is my eye first drawn?
- Where does it move to next?
- What creates depth in the frame?
- What effect does the use of light have in the frame?
- What effect does movement to and from the lens have?
- What effect does any movement across and through the frame have?
- What effect does the movement of the frame have?
- Is part of the frame filled by an object or some architecture? What effect does this have?

You can train yourself to understand the impact of different ways of framing. The most important thing is to regularly look at the world – and dancing bodies – through the viewfinder of your camera.

The rectangle creates a cone

If you hold a camera still and look through the lens at a dancer moving around a space, you will notice that they disappear from view at certain points.

If you then mark out the boundaries of when the dancer is in frame and when he or she disappears, you will discover that a triangle shape is created on the floor, with the narrowest point starting below the centre of the lens.

If you then ask the dancer to move towards, then away from the camera, you also notice that the closer the dancer comes to the lens, the less of his or her body is visible in the frame. As the dancer moves away from the lens, more of their body comes into shot, until there is point at which the entire height of their body can be seen in the frame.

Any movement away from the camera from that point, and more space will become visible above, below and beside them. Any movement closer in towards the lens, and their head and feet will disappear again.

This shows you that what was a triangle on the floor is actually a cone shape, fanning out in three dimensions from the centre of the lens.

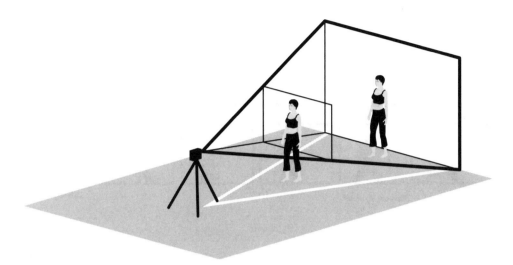

Figure 2.2 **The rectangle creates a cone**

It is essential for anyone making video dance to know about this so-called 'cone-effect'. It forms the basis of the contrast between how space is perceived on the screen, as opposed to on the stage.

An understanding of this characteristic of the lens and its effect on movement in and through the frame must inform how choreography is created for the camera and how the camera is positioned in relationship to the dance.

Being able to visualise and work with this cone shape is something that develops the more you work. Soon you will also have an instinctive sense of what the camera will and will not see at a certain point, without even having to look through the lens all the time.

The frame becomes a shot

Another important point to understand when thinking about the frame is that it will rarely remain the same for more than a split second. Either the camera or the subject of the frame – and most often both – will inevitably be in motion, continually reshaping the frame, thereby altering its design and what it communicates.

It is the effect of a series of continually altering frames that makes up what we call a 'shot'. A shot has duration, whereas a frame is a moment caught in time.

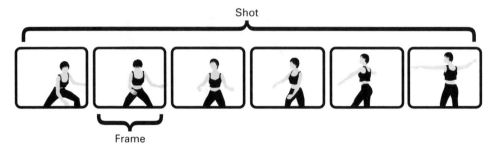

Figure 2.3 **The frames become a shot**

How to describe a shot

Video dance-making usually involves many different people working together and sharing a vision of what is being created. The communication of that vision is essential, and therefore it is useful to use a shared vocabulary to describe what the camera sees and how it is framed.

The terms most commonly used to describe shot types define how the camera positions the viewer in relation to the subject of the frame. For example, in a 'wide-shot', the subject is framed with space around it. This creates the impression that the viewer is standing back from the subject, taking a wide view. A 'close-up' implies that the viewer is positioned close to the subject, with the subject filling the frame.

Page 29 shows a list of shot types and how their names are shortened when written. Figure 2.4 shows how these shots may look relative to each other.

Figure 2.4 (opposite): **Shot types and their descriptions**

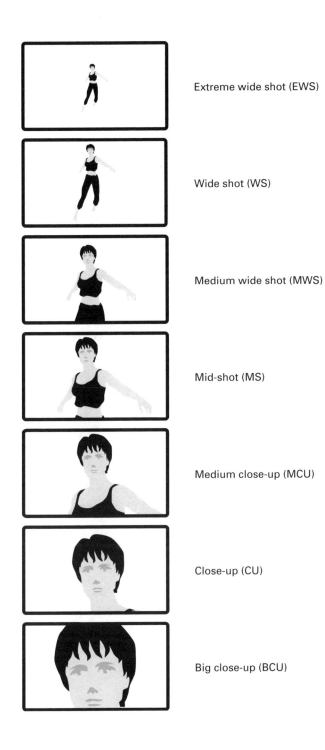

Extreme wide shot (EWS)

Wide shot (WS)

Medium wide shot (MWS)

Mid-shot (MS)

Medium close-up (MCU)

Close-up (CU)

Big close-up (BCU)

Tip!

Shot sizes are relative to each other. What is described as a wide shot in one video dance might be a close-up in another, depending on its context within the work.

Some characteristics of shot sizes

The precise nature of different shot sizes and how they are read by the viewer will depend on their usage within your video dance, that is, what fills the frame and how the shots are edited together.

However, different types of shot do have certain characteristics that are useful to consider.

- A wide shot places the subject of your frame – that is, the dancer or dancers – in a context, as it allows you to see where their action is taking place.
- A mid-shot shows the action more clearly by bringing the viewer in closer to the dancer or dancers.
- A close-up conveys effort, emotion, texture or movement quality by focusing on a detail of the face or body.

As we will explore in greater depth when we look at creative editing techniques in Chapter 9, it is important to film a good range and variety of shot sizes, for it is by placing contrasting shots together that you create energy, interest, rhythm and pace in your work. Overall, however, favouring closer shots over wider ones when filming and editing exploits the real potential of video dance and opens up compelling opportunities unique to dance on screen.

'The slight raise of an eyebrow is such a small movement, but can be so big and say so much on camera. That's what's so wonderful about making dance for the screen.'

Liz Aggiss, director/choreographer

Camera position

As well as the size of the shot, the position of the camera offers many choices. The camera can place the viewer almost anywhere in relation to the dance. Depending on the camera position, the movement can be framed from:

- in front
- behind

- below
- any diagonal angle.
- above

Positions such as directly overhead ('bird's-eye') or directly below ('worm's-eye') create extreme viewpoints on the dance.

Explore the possibilities yourself by looking through the lens and changing your position in relation to what you are filming. You will notice that even very subtle changes of camera position alter greatly the framing of an image, its affect and what that communicates. (See Figures 2.5 and 2.6.)

The camera in motion

Because the subject of the frame is human movement, video dance invites – even demands – the camera to be in motion. How the camera moves in relation to the dancer or dancers, and the space they are in, has great impact on the viewer's experience of the movement.

The movement of the camera through space means that what the lens sees will change and, as a result, the framing of the shot will continually alter.

One of my priorities when directing video dance is to make the viewer feel like they are involved in the dance, and I have found that the best way of doing this is to include plenty of camera movement in the filming.

This is something that you have to experience for yourself and is easy to try out. You can ask a dancer to improvise for you and look through the lens as you move with your camera through the space.

How does your camera move?

There are essentially two different types of camera movement.

1. The body of the camera itself remains fixed in space (often placed on a tripod), whilst the lens moves. For example, the lens can move sideways, either left or right, to create a horizontal camera movement called 'panning'. Or it can move up and down, to create

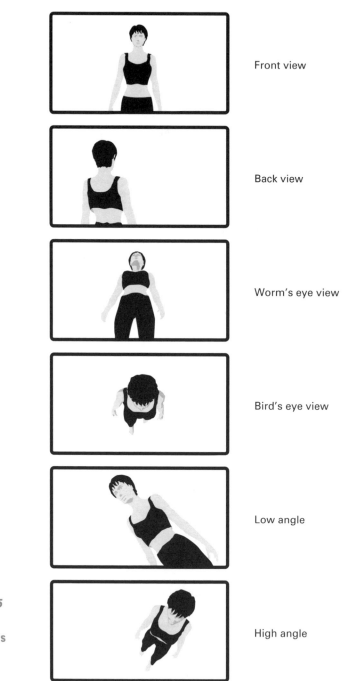

Front view

Back view

Worm's eye view

Bird's eye view

Low angle

Figure 2.5
**Various
viewpoints
on the
dance**

High angle

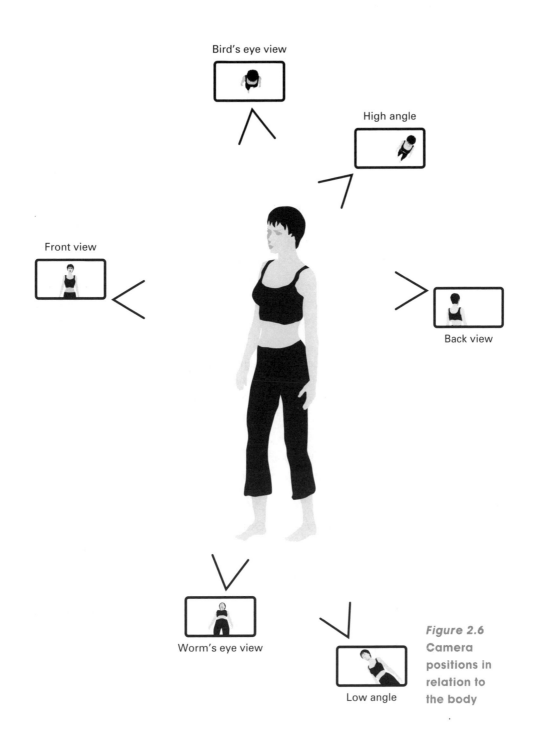

Bird's eye view

High angle

Front view

Back view

Worm's eye view

Low angle

Figure 2.6
**Camera
positions in
relation to
the body**

a vertical movement called 'tilting'. The fixed camera can also 'roll' (turning everything in its vision upside down and then upright again), although this action is easiest tried out holding the camera in your hand.

2. Movement can also be created by the camera travelling through space.

- The camera can move towards, or away from an object or person.
- Alternatively, it can move past or around an object or person.

Movement through space of the camera is usually referred to as 'tracking'. This term derives from the fact that, in order to achieve smooth and constant motion, the camera is often placed on a trolley with wheels, which is then positioned on rails like small train tracks.

Tracking-shots can be used to reveal the location in which you are filming, by travelling through the space. This effect is enhanced if the camera passes close to features of the architecture – for example, a pillar or a doorway.

Another type of camera movement is a zoom, either in or out. This closing in or opening out of the lens through various different angles is usually used to reframe a shot closer or wider, but the movement itself can also be incorporated into the actual shot.

The zoom action can also be added into other types of camera movement. For example, you can chose to zoom in as the camera tracks forward, or zoom out as the camera tracks back.

Terms used to describe camera movement

pan	camera on a fixed point, the lens moves left or right on the horizontal plane
tilt	camera on a fixed point, the lens moves up or down on the vertical plane
track	camera moves through space in any direction
crib	camera moves up or down through space on the vertical plane
whip-pan	a very fast pan

zoom   camera on a fixed point, the lens closes in on, or widens out from, the subject of the frame

crash zoom   a very fast zoom

Filming for the edit

Understanding the different ways that the camera can frame the subject and move in relation to the action is fundamental to making video dance.

As part of this, however, you must also consider how the work is going to be edited. This is because, ultimately, all filming is about creating material for the edit. This is where your video dance will be given the shape that defines it.

Unlike in the theatre, where each audience member will normally only watch the dance from one position for the duration of a performance, in video dance, the perspective on the action is continually altered by cutting between shots that offer different views and framing of the dance.

Therefore, how you plan to then place these shots together should inform your approach to filming and guide you in your choices. This is very important, not least because when you finally reach the editing stage, it will be difficult, if not impossible, to go back and shoot what you now realise that you need.

The detail with which you plan the edit in advance is a matter of preference.

- Some people like to know exactly what shot will be placed next to which before they start filming and they storyboard meticulously.
- Others take a more fluid approach, filming very specific material, conscious of the range of different shots they will need, but with a more open mind as to the exact structure of the final edit.
- And some people mix both approaches, depending on the nature and intention of the different sections of their video dance.

We will look at different ways of developing your video dance material, and storyboarding in the next chapter. But first, let's look at some of the fundamental concepts behind editing.

Approaches to space and time

When you begin to think about how your video dance will be edited, it is useful to consider that there are basically two contrasting approaches.

1. Filming to maintain the continuity of the live choreography.
2. The 'montage' approach, in which the live choreography is completely reordered in the edit suite.

Both have much in common in terms of production processes, use of camera, sound and the finer details of editing. The main difference lies in the treatment of time and space.

Continuity

Filming for the continuity of the choreography means that your video dance maintains the same structure as the live choreography. The term 'continuity' refers to the fact that, in the final video dance, the choreography will appear to run in sequence, with one movement following the other, as it would if you were watching it on a stage in front of you.

The basic process of filming for the continuity of the live choreography is as follows.

*   A piece of choreography is created.
*   This is filmed in its entirety, with a variety of shots providing different framing and angles on the dancers' movement.
*   In the edit, these shots are laid down in the order that recreates exactly the structure of the choreography.

Cutting between the different types of shots generates interest and energy on the screen, by allowing the viewer to see certain moments in close-up detail, with wider shots showing the relationship between the dancers or the spatial context of the dance.

It is important that each moment of the choreography is filmed in at least one shot, in order that the shape of the movement as it existed live can be translated onto the screen.

In the continuity approach, the music to which the live choreography was performed usually becomes the soundtrack to the video dance, with the relationship between the dancers' movement and the music being retained. Here again, you must ensure that you have shots covering all the choreography, otherwise you may find yourself without the right images to accompany certain bars or phrases of the music.

Filming for the continuity of the choreography is frequently used when the purpose is to make a documentation of a live performance, whether that is in front of an audience, or restaged in a studio at a later date.

Montage

In the 'montage approach' to editing, any sense of what happened 'for real' is abandoned, as the material that has been filmed is reordered, creating video dance choreography that is unique to the screen.

Watch any feature film and you will see that the montage approach is central to the language of cinema. Whilst occasionally a scene may cover a sequence of action step by step, that is, using the continuity approach described earlier, far the more widespread is the creation of action and meaning through montage.

Picture this, for example: a car drives up and stops in front of a house. Cut to a shot from inside a living room, as a man appears through the door.

The implication is that the man has got out of the car, opened the gate, walked up to the front door, opened it and gone into the house, down the hall and into the sitting room. But we don't need to see shots of all this action. As viewers, our brains make sense of the images we are given by filling in the gaps, and we can imagine the sequence of events in between. In fact, if we were shown every moment of this action, in real time, it would make for very dull viewing.

On another level, single shots of apparently unrelated events or objects will create meaning through being 'montaged' together. For example, a shot of an empty plate on a table, followed by a close-up of a dog licking its lips, will read as the dog having eaten the dinner.

In video dance, it is through montage editing that you can break away from any concept of choreography as it happened 'live' and think alternatively about time and space, as they are perceived on screen.

Shots featuring completely different sequences of choreography, in various locations, with contrasting costumes, design and even different dancers can be juxtaposed to create original screen choreography. What will link them is the overall theme of the work and the judgement and skill with which the images are edited together.

Montage approach can also be used with shots that come from the same source: for example, a section of choreography, filmed in one location, yet offering a completely different experience of space and time.

Not bound by what is possible in a live context, the repetition of images and sound can take montage in video dance into a new dimension, and completely alter the viewer's perspective on dance.

In the context of making video dance, it is the montage approach that takes us into a new realm of creativity. This is not to deny the value of beautifully directed screen versions of live works using the continuity approach. But, if video dance is to continue to develop as an art form in its own right, related to but not restrained by what is possible in live dance performance, then the montage approach needs to be understood, embraced and exploited.

Exercises

All the exercises in this chapter require a video camera, tripod, at least one dancer and a suitable studio or location. You may find it useful to have some short sequences of movement already taught to the dancers to use as a starting point for the screen choreography.

Still frame

- Set up your camera on a tripod.
- Zoom the lens out to its widest angle and design a frame. Remember, the camera can be positioned at any height or angle and need not be facing the middle of the space.

- Now create a video dance of between 1 and 3 minutes duration by choreographing the dancers in this frame.

You may not change the shot in any way, for example, by moving the camera, but the dancers can move in, out and through the shot.

The challenge is to explore the characteristics of space in front of camera, how the lens effects our perception of space and motion, and how creatively a static frame can be used.

Develop and rehearse your short video dance before recording it. A few takes may be required until you achieve the one that you are happy with.

If part of a workshop, after an allotted time, it can be interesting to watch each group's selected 'best' version and to share comments and feedback with the class.

Some additions and alternatives:

- You can do some animation-style editing by stopping and restarting the recording and altering things in the frame whilst the camera is on pause. But do not move the camera!
- Create an instant soundtrack to your piece by adding an audio element to your choreographed shot, for example someone singing off camera or the dancers creating sounds as they move.

Moving camera/single shot

Choreograph and film a minute-long continuous shot involving one or more dancers and in which the camera is in constant motion for the duration.

The camera movement can be the result of panning, tilting and zooming or tracking and combinations thereof. For flexibility, handhold the camera or carry it on your shoulder.

In-camera montage

1.

Choreograph and film a video dance made up of the following shots in the order that they appear below:

WS, MCU, BCU, MS, WS, CU, MWS, BCU, WS, CU

You need to 'edit in camera', which means that the shots must be filmed consecutively. You should rehearse each different shot before recording, as you only want one take of each shot on tape. By the end of the exercise, you will have created a montage sequence.

Once filming is complete, look back at what you have filmed and analyse the effect of the juxtaposition of the different types of shots and, if working in a group, look at each group's version and discuss whether each shot has the characteristic you would expect.

2.

Now make a video dance that includes the following shots, but this time you can choose the order that they come in and to which shot size you will also apply the directions for camera movement.

Edit in camera as before, rehearsing and then filming only one take of each shot:

2 x WS, 1 x BCU, 3 X CU, 2 x MCU, 2 x MS, 1 x track, 2 x pan, 1 x tilt

CONTENTS

CHAPTER 3

Developing the Work

Having been introduced to some concepts of camera and movement, it is now time to look in detail at the transformation of your video dance, from the initial idea to the first frame that is filmed on the shoot.

This stage of the process is called 'pre-production' and involves various activities, including finding locations and preparing costumes as well as assembling a crew, booking equipment, and devising schedules and storyboards.

Evolving a way of working that suits your particular project is essential, and what you read in the next few chapters can help with this. And because the performance of the dancers is at the heart of what video dance communicates, the development of the choreography is the best place to start.

Choreography for the camera

A question that often arises at this early stage is which comes first, the choreography or the shot? Or, to put it another way, at what point in the process of making your video dance should you start working with a camera in rehearsal?

As always, this will depend on the nature of your idea and the intention of the work. If you are creating a video dance based on an already existing live work, then you will have the body of choreography that you can immediately look at through the camera lens and begin to decide how you want to film.

If you are starting from scratch, you may decide that it is best to create some choreography for the dancers, based on the idea for your video dance, before involving the camera in the process.

Alternatively, you may feel that the choreography of both dancers and camera should be evolved simultaneously, perhaps by using some of the improvisation techniques described later on in this chapter.

The way that you choose to work may also vary depending on whether you are both choreographing and directing, or if you are working as a choreographer/director team, or any other type of collaboration. It is also very much about personal preference, and this can change from project to project. There are, however, some essential thoughts that are useful to consider.

'As I create movement for a video dance work, I am always thinking about where it will be filmed from and on what scale. I can't create movement without knowing how it will be seen. If I start to make movement from no particular point of view, I will have to rework it when I have decided.'

Lea Anderson, choreographer

'Choreography for the camera' can be a rather misleading phrase. Yes, the movement may have been specially created for the screen, but it also needs an additional intention, whether that is expressive or formal, or a combination of both.

This is as much to do with the structure of the work as it is to do with what it is communicating. If the sole purpose of the choreography is to fill the frame with movement, you will end up with carefully designed shots, but it will be hard to edit them together effectively.

This is because, as we will explore in greater depth in Chapter 9, editing requires movement through the frame to create energy and to draw the eye from one shot to the next. If this is lacking, because the choreographed action begins and ends within the frame, it results in an unsatisfying lack of fluidity.

There is sometimes also the misconception that choreographing for the camera means that you should make movement that 'fits' into the parameters of the frame.

The opposite is true for, as we saw in Chapter 2, it is often the effect of only seeing a fragment of the dancer or the dancer's movement that creates the on-screen energy.

This happens, for example, when the lens is framed in a close-up, focusing on a part of the body and when the dancer moves through frame, or a combination of both. The reason that this creates a sense of energy is down to the fact that as the viewer sees only a part of the action, their mind will be working to recreate or imagine the rest of the movement. It makes for an active kind of viewing.

Similarly, through close-up framing, you can experience the effect that a whole body movement has on a particular part of a dancer's body. For example, whilst the dancer may be circling his or her torso round, the camera may frame the side of the waist, revealing the effort and the quality of the action through the detail of the action. Very often, this type of shot will express much more about the movement than a wide shot featuring the entire body in motion.

So, we see that choreographing for the camera does not necessarily mean every step being created whilst looking down the lens. In fact, the initial process of developing material can be made a lot easier if there is some movement created for the dancers first, that the camera can then respond to and alter. The trick is that whoever is choreographing should understand how the lens can affect the perception of movement and, of course, be clear about the intention of the work.

Creating choreography on location

'None of the dancing in *boy* could really exist as separate movement because it's so tied up with the environment. Whether it's a jump, or it's just picking up a handful of sand, or it's running along a dune! We always prefer to work in the environment rather than do too much development in the studio before hand.'

Rosemary Lee, choreographer/director

As well as deciding at what point in the process you want to start looking through the lens, it is also important to consider when you will start to work on location and its effect on the creation of the choreography.

As we will discuss in greater detail in Chapter 4, the potential to take dance into new and diverse environments is one of the greatest appeals of video dance, both to the artist and to the viewer. It also presents some of the greatest challenges.

For the majority of live works, the transition from rehearsal studio to stage is relatively simple, at least in terms of the environment that the dancers are used to performing in and the type of floor that the movement is choreographed on.

In the video dance-making process, the shift from rehearsal studio to location can be dramatic and unforgiving. Imagine, for example, the implications for the dancers of creating and rehearsing an energetic and acrobatic duet on a sprung wooden floor in a heated room, only to find that it is to be filmed on the concrete stairs in an underground car park at night!

In most cases, the ideal scenario would be to choreograph and rehearse each section in the location in which it is to be filmed, but this is often impractical and/or beyond the scope of the budget.

However, if your location has extreme features that will inevitably form an integral part of the choreography, you must do everything possible to enable as much development and rehearsal to take place *in situ*. The effort will pay off.

A common, and often most the feasible, solution is to spend a short time at the beginning of the creative process at the location of your choice with your core team and a camera.

This way you can all experience the place for real, be inspired, see what is possible and generate ideas that can then be taken back into the studio. There the work of choreographing the dancers and camera can continue, informed by everyone's experiences of the location.

'Often you don't know what it's really going to be like until you are on location. There can be a certain awkwardness in the movement because the performer is, say, running along a path with roots all over it and they're bound to trip and there's only so fast they can run. Everything changes all the time working on location and I find that incredibly frustrating, but also magical. I think change is inherent to film-making and it is part of my life challenge to figure out how to cope with it.'

Laura Taler, choreographer/director

Approaches to filming dance

In many respects, how you choose to develop your video dance material depends on your attitude to how it is going to be filmed on the actual shoot. Here are two contrasting approaches.

1. The dancer is asked to perform short sections of the choreography and the director specifically designs one or more shots (for example, CU, WS, Bird's eye, tracking shot, etc.) for each of these movement sections. The fluidity of the dance as seen on the screen is then created through editing, by the way that the individual shots are placed next to the other.
2. The dancer is allowed to perform longer sections of movement, maintaining the integrity of the choreographic flow. The director develops approaches to filming these longer sections based on the overall intent of the video dance. These longer pieces of footage can then be broken down into shorter clips in the edit.

Neither of the above approaches means that, when it comes to the edit, the continuity of the live choreography is necessarily recreated, as was discussed in Chapter 2. What is important here is the method of filming. The actual structuring of the material in the edit is still wide open to your imagination and dependent on the aims of your video dance.

Tip!

It is crucial that
you abandon any
sense of 'front',
'upstage' and
'downstage'.
You must try
to think about
space as three-
dimensional
and realise that
the camera can
take the viewer
anywhere
around – and
even inside
– the dance.

In the former approach, the filming process is a very stop-start experience for the dancer, but it can yield excellent results as exact positions in the frame can be achieved.

In the latter approach, the dancer's energy is paramount. However, what is gained in terms of the freedom for the dancer may be lost in the precision of the framing of each shot and a more fluid use of camera must come into play.

But taking this second approach does not mean that you should resort to a safe way of filming, with everything filmed in wide or mid-shots in order that you have a chance to get something in the frame. The filming can and must be as inventive as ever. The big difference is that the movement captured will be in full flow and will have a sense of momentum of its own.

Whatever approach you take – and you may well combine both – you must be prepared to work hard to achieve what you want. Don't resort to indistinct shots that capture 'everything' just because you are not brave enough to make radical decisions about framing or because the logistics seem too difficult.

Contrasting needs

As soon as you begin to think in any detail about the requirements of dance and video as separate creative processes, you realise that they are in fact uncomfortable partners.

The power of the camera is based very much on the design of each shot. Even a slight alteration in the relationship between the frame and its contents can alter radically the nature of a shot and what it communicates.

When filming dance, in order to ensure that a carefully planned camera movement is achieved or a certain light comes into play, the dancer is often required to reach certain fixed points in space. This can affect his or her ability to perform by restricting the flow of movement.

Such detailed work demands precision, and it is often necessary to film the same shot over and over again until it is right and until exactly what is needed for the edit has been captured.

In contrast, dance depends for its expression on a certain amount of spontaneity in the moment of performance and a sense of momentum as the dancer moves through space (unless the aim of the choreography is to represent an image of restricted movement).

Whilst the ability to reach a certain 'spot' on stage is a skill that any theatre performer must learn, in filming video dance, the challenges are even greater. When the requirements of a specific frame combine with the demands of the lighting and often, a dance-unfriendly location, the dancer's ability to perform is often severely compromised.

Added to this is the fact that, no matter how fit, dancers are human beings with a finite amount of energy and focus. This means that there are only so many times that a movement or sequence can be repeated for the camera before tiredness sets in, affecting performance and, crucially, making injury more likely.

So, you can see, video dance has some great challenges inherent in its hybrid form. However, don't be put off by these difficulties. All that is necessary is to understand the issues involved and to make well-considered decisions on how you want to work, based on the aims and priorities of your own particular video dance project and the people with whom you are collaborating.

My own approach

When I started off making video dance, I would carefully design and storyboard each shot according to the intention of the individual work. When it came to the shoot, the dancers, cameraperson and I would painstakingly recreate and film each shot.

This material would then be pieced together in the edit suite and combined with sound to create video dance works that explored framing, pace, rhythm and repetition. What I gradually began to realise, however, was that the dancers with whom I was working never had the chance to really move for the camera, to rush, turn, spin or jump through space.

This led me to start to explore various different uses of improvisation within the video dance-making process and has opened up completely new ways of working to me and the many dance artists with whom I have collaborated.

Over time, I have developed an approach to making video dance that exploits the benefits of improvisation. It is an approach that I feel has much to offer, whether you use improvisation as part of a development process or as a means of generating the actual material that will be used in your completed video dance work. It is worth, therefore, spending some time exploring the subject.

Mutual performers: improvisation in the video dance-making process

First of all, let's consider what we mean by improvisation.

Looking it up in the *Collins' English Dictionary*, I find the Latin root of the word 'improvisation' is '*improvisus*', meaning 'unforeseen'. *Collins* gives the definition of the word as 'composing as you go'. Both these terms shed interesting light on the practice.

If you come from a dance background, then you will be aware that improvisation is used widely, both as a tool for developing new movement that can then be fixed as set choreography and as a performance activity in its own right.

Within my own video dance-making practice, improvisation has meant using preconceived instructions or 'scores' to generate material, informed by the theme of the work and the needs of each particular scene. This material can then be developed and set as repeatable choreography for the dancers and specific framing and movement of the camera.

Using improvisation as part of the video dance-making process has many benefits. It can:

- generate new ideas, as the starting point for a video dance work might be inspired by images that are created through improvisation
- build an understanding of the many ways in which dance and camera can interact and the effect of the dancers' movement in relation to the camera's framing, position and movement
- increase awareness of the characteristics of the camera – for example, the impact of different framing, lenses and camera movements on the perception of movement

- help dancers and the cameraperson to gain confidence, moving together in what is often a confined space and in close proximity
- encourage collaboration and communication between a creative team – dancers, choreographer, cameraperson, director – as they work together to create, look at, analyse and consider exploring ways of developing the improvised material.

Improvisation on the shoot

Whilst it is widely accepted that improvisation is a valid tool for generating ideas and developing material for video dance, when it comes to filming the material that is to be used in the edited work, it is usually thought to be wiser to set and rehearse everything before committing to tape.

However, if a considered and structured approach is taken, improvisation can be an excellent way of generating the actual material that will form part, or the whole, of your edited video dance.

Improvised material has been used in a number of the video dance works that I have directed. In some cases, this has been for certain sections – for example, in *Moment*, where around 20 per cent of the material was improvised, with the remainder being set. In other works, such as *Pace* and *Sense-8*, all the material was generated through structured improvisations on the shoot.

There is a qualitative difference between the performance of video dance material that has been set exactly and material that retains elements of improvisation. We have already touched on the benefits of allowing a sense of freedom and spontaneity in the dancer's performance; improvisation on the shoot enables these important qualities to become part of the final work.

Be warned, however, that if you are planning to try and raise funds to make your work, for some commissioners of video dance the fact that you plan to work with improvisation to generate your material may be a scary concept and one which they feel they cannot support. To the uninitiated, the word 'improvisation' suggests a free for all of unprepared filming, with everyone doing what they please and then seeing what can be pieced together in the edit suite.

As we will now explore, this is not at all what using improvisation properly within a video dance-making context means. In fact, the opposite is true, but you cannot expect everyone to understand this. So, if you want to openly pursue this process, then you need to be extra clear of the intention of your work, be more than prepared and have all the arguments ready to defend!

Creating and using a score

There are different ways of working with improvisation in video dance. For example, you can:

- ask a dancer to perform set choreographed movement whilst the camera improvises
- establish the camera movement, and then ask the dancer to improvise
- have both dancer and camera improvise.

In all cases, however, rather than simply saying, 'OK then, please start to dance and film', the idea is to develop a 'score' that will guide the improvisation. A score can provide:

- a starting point
- an idea to work with
- a set of rules
- guidance on how to move and what to frame.

A score is basically a set of guidelines, rules or challenges agreed at the beginning of the improvisation that those involved – the dancer and camera operator – are asked to follow.

For example, a simple 'score' for a video dance improvisation might be:

The dancer improvises on the words 'swoop', 'fall' and 'stillness'. The camera is on a track that is laid in a circle around the space in which the dancer is dancing. The camera circles around the dancer, anti-clockwise and at a steady pace, gradually changing shot sizes as it goes.

From experience, I can predict the type of video dance material that will be generated by the score described. What I don't know is how exactly it will be interpreted by the individual dancer, or by the cameraperson.

How to develop a score

One of the exciting things about working with improvisation in video dance is that you can develop your own scores.

You can start with an idea or concept that you want to work with. It may be the essential idea behind your video dance work, or it may be something that fits into a particular scene or section of the work.

The score can be based on a concept that you want to follow through and see where it takes you.

Alternatively, it can be designed to achieve a certain quality or relationship that you are aiming for, drawn from your understanding of the effect of certain elements coming together.

For example, if you ask the dancer to improvise around the words: 'flight' 'stretch' and 'soft', you will have in your head a certain image of the type of movement that will result.

There are many ways that these words could be interpreted, and the exact nature of the movement will depend on who is improvising, the context in which they are moving and how they feel in the moment. The great joy and thrill of working with improvisation is that it allows each dancer to bring their own response and interpretation to the process.

Similarly, you can give the cameraperson a 'score'. This could be as straightforward as asking them only to move the camera in a certain way, or to try to achieve a certain quality of movement, or to focus on a particular aspect of the dancers' bodies in motion.

The score for the camera could be something like this:

> With the camera on the tripod and the lens zoomed in halfway, pan left and right on the horizontal plane.

This might seem very prescriptive, but what remains for the camera operator is to find the rhythm and speed of the camera movement, in relation to how he or she sees the dancers move in and through the frame. Believe me, it leaves plenty of latitude for personal input.

An important thing to know is that the material that you will create by using improvisation on the shoot will tend to be in short fragments.

When dancer and camera are improvising, the times when everything converges to create the kind of images that you are looking for may be fleeting, especially when filming in close-up and with a moving camera. Your work as you prepare to edit at a later stage will be to find these precious moments amongst all the material filmed.

Some people might say: 'Why bother with improvisation on the shoot? Why not decide exactly what you want and then set it as repeatable choreography and camera movement?' The answer is, using improvisation on the shoot, if properly conceived and well prepared, can yield the most perfect and exciting moments of video dance, full of energy, excitement and with a sense of aliveness that is hard to achieve in any other way.

Some practical considerations about improvisation

I hope that you will feel inspired to try out improvisation as an approach to making video dance. Here are some practical tips that I have picked up in the course of working in this way.

Make sure everyone involved in an improvisation is clear about the rules or 'score'.

Define the area of space in which the dancers and camera are to move. This will be determined by the nature of your location, what you do and do not want to see in frame and, importantly, the light.

It is best to set a time limit for each improvisation, because when exciting material begins to unfold in front of your eyes, it is easy to exhaust people by letting things run and run.

Always find a gentle way of bringing an improvisation to an end. Rather than shouting 'cut' in the middle of a wonderful movement, warn the improvisers that the planned time is up and that they should find a way to end their dance.

You can improvise with the camera on a tripod, on a track or handheld. As always, this is dependent on the effect that you want to create. A more detailed description of grip equipment and its use is to be found in Chapter 7.

When filming an improvisation, you do not necessarily know exactly what the camera will be seeing at any given moment. Therefore, you need to make sure that anything that you don't want to appear in shot is removed from the space.

You may also have to ask anyone who is not essential to filming to leave the space for the duration of the take. That will most likely be everyone apart from the cameraperson, the director and the sound recordist. Those remaining, and who are not meant to be in shot, will now have to perform an unseen and silent dance behind the camera, as they try and stay out of shot whilst doing their job.

If you are not operating the camera yourself, you may choose to leave the camera operator and dancers to get on with the improvisation alone. This will give them the space that they need. Ask them to call you in when they feel that they have achieved what you are setting out to do, or they are experiencing problems, or they need a break.

After each improvisation, look back and assess what was filmed. This is a very beneficial process, especially if you involve the dancers and camera operator in the process. If your collaborators are aware of what you are trying to achieve, then their input can be enormous.

If you are planning to ask the dancers to get up and move again, make sure that they do not cool down too much whilst they are viewing the material.

Remember that when looking through the lens of a camera it is easy to lose awareness of what is happening around you and to misjudge distances. In all cases, work as closely as you can with the idea whilst avoiding any danger of hurting anyone. As the director, safety on the shoot (and in rehearsals involving the camera) is your responsibility and you must do everything that you can to make sure nobody gets hurt.

The aim is not necessarily to achieve long, continuous shots that 'work' all the way through. As has been mentioned – and as we will look at more closely in Chapter 9 – fleeting moments can provide the material for your montage editing.

Developing your own use of camera

Whatever process you have followed to develop your work as regards the dancers' movement and the way it is filmed, there comes a point at which you must consolidate what has been evolved and begin to prepare for the actual shoot.

When working with a choreographer who is creating movement material with dancers in the rehearsal studio, I find that there is a clear progression in the way the work evolves.

To begin with, I work freely and instinctively, looking at the dancers' movement through the camera and experimenting with different framing, lens sizes, camera positions and movement.

As I look – recording most of the time so that my collaborators and I can view the material later – I follow up possibilities that suggest themselves. All the time, I keep in mind the central idea of the work and this, combined with the effect of seeing the dancers' performance through the lens, informs the choices I make as to what to film and how to move the camera.

Over time – this will depend on the scale of the work and the length of the rehearsal period – I begin to hone down the possibilities and to make decisions about the way that different sections of movement might be filmed. Uppermost in my mind is the fact that the editor will always be looking for a variety of frames, movement and shot sizes. Whilst planning, I make lots of notes and sketch floor plans detailing camera positions and movement.

Often this is a very collaborative process with the choreographers and dancers. We will look at the rehearsal footage together on a monitor in the studio and discuss what is evolving in relation to the idea for the work.

Sometimes, to help the process, I do an edit of what I have filmed, either simply laying off shots that I particularly like to share with my collaborators in no particular order. Or I edit in more detail, using this to help me work out an overall structure for the work or specific approaches that might be taken in different sections.

By the time the shoot comes, I will know exactly how all (or almost all) the material is to be filmed. Part of this will be about working out how much time we have on the shoot and what is achievable. We look at the scheduling of filming days in Chapter 5.

Storyboarding

'What I have learnt is that most of dance filming is about pencil and paper and I never, ever go into any project not being fully prepared. Whether that's a single camera, five-minute video dance or a big huge multi-camera recording, I've thought through every single shot. Now, sometimes things don't work out as planned, but I have always thought the film through in my brain to prove to myself that it works.'

Ross MacGibbon, director

Part of the clarification and preparation process involves creating a storyboard and/or a shot list.

Storyboarding is a detailed method of representing what it is that you are planning to film in terms of the frame and its content, and it should be designed so that it is as useful as possible to your particular project.

A well-conceived storyboard can:

- give you an overview of your video dance, which can help you to work out if you have planned for what you need, if there are obvious gaps, or sections that could become 'optional' if you run out of time
- help you to work out your daily shooting schedules, as well as the all-important logistics of a particularly complex scene or series of shots or frames
- be the focal point of planning discussions between you and your creative team, including the choreographer, lighting cameraperson and production designer.

On the actual shoot, you can use your storyboard to remind yourself how you had planned to film the material. This is a vital tool, as it is easy to lose your way, with so many people around you and with a constantly evolving situation and questions coming at you from every angle.

Tip!

Give each section of video dance material that is developed in rehearsal a name, as this helps dancers and crew to know immediately which part of the material you are talking about. Sections in video dance works that I have directed have had names like 'Observational', 'Triangle' and 'Grab Onto'.

Conventionally, a storyboard is a set of drawings, rather like a cartoon strip, that represents the shots that you plan to film, placed in the order in which you anticipate that they will be edited together.

Other options are to draw stick figures and diagrams or to write out descriptions of the different shots. A storyboard can also include photographic or video images, or a mixture of all these techniques.

My own preference is for making floor plans of the location and marking where the dancers and cameras will be positioned and will move in different sections of the dance. I then write lists with detailed notes on all the shots, or the improvisation scores, that I want to film. I find that this approach works better for my own approach to filming than sketching out a series of specific frames, not least because I can't really draw!

'I storyboard when I am working with a crew and I want to know how many shots I need to accomplish that day, because I need to have a schedule, and because I need to tell other people about what we are doing. I want to be able to say at the beginning of the day, "We have six shots today, and we're doing this, and this, and this, and this . . ." because it helps people to make a connection with you as a film-maker.'

Elliot Caplan, director

Exercises

For the improvisation exercises, you will need a camera, a suitable space (a dance studio is often easiest to begin with until you and your team's confidence grows) and at least one dancer. The storyboarding exercise only requires paper and pencil, but it is helpful to have some choreography (filmed as a wide shot) as a memory aide, or an actual video dance, or filmed exercise to base it on.

Video dance improvisations

Taking guidance from what you have read in this chapter, why not try out the following suggestions for video dance improvisations.

1.

Take a choreographed duet. Swap in the camera with one of the dancers, adapting the choreography to incorporate the camera. What the camera sees (and shoots) is from the perspective of the dancer who has stepped out. After some rehearsal, record and look back at the results. The aim is to create a single-shot video dance; however, you can also try in-camera editing, if you prefer.

2.

Try the above exercise again, but this time place another solo dancer in the space. The camera should maintain its focus as above, but will glimpse the other action peripherally. Again, you can create a single shot, or edit in camera. When watching back, notice the effect that the added dancer has on your perception of space as depicted on the screen.

3.

Either set an improvisation or choreograph a solo for one dancer. The person operating the camera tries to keep the dancer's face in frame. As the dancer moves, the camera will also be forced to move. Sometimes the dancer will disappear out of the frame – the camera operator must simply try and reframe on the face, whilst at the same time making the shot as interesting and 'usable' as possible.

4.

As (3), but now choose a body part to frame and follow. You can either be very specific (for example, left shoulder) or can be slightly looser (shoulders, waist, etc). By all means try feet, but it is the obvious one!

Within each of the above improvisations, there are many different options that will change the look and feel of the material being created. For example,

- Try one of the improvisations with the camera lens zoomed out to its widest.
- Then try the same one again, but this time with the lens zoomed half way in.

With all the improvisations, it is a good idea to watch them back after a few attempts and to decide what works for you and what doesn't. If you wish, from there you can start to set the choreography of either the camera or the dancer, or both.

5.

Develop your own video dance score, according to your own interests and context. Refer back to what is written in this chapter for advice on using improvisation as a creative tool. The material that you generate can be used when you are exploring editing at a later stage.

Storyboarding

Create a storyboard based on the video dance that you filmed for the 'moving camera/single shot' or the 'in-camera montage' exercises in Chapter 2.

It is up to you to devise the most suitable approach to take, according to the nature of the material that you are storyboarding. You can also create a storyboard based on the treatment that you wrote as part of the exercises at the end of Chapter 1.

CONTENTS

CHAPTER 4

Creating your on-screen world

One of the many challenges of making video dance is that there is nowhere to hide. Every dot on the screen and every fraction of a second matters, as the viewer takes in all that they hear and see, whether consciously or not.

This can mean several things, not least that making 5 minutes of video dance can be as time- and energy-consuming as creating a 40-minute-long live dance work.

It also means that everything that goes into creating each moment of your video dance must be carefully considered. Included in this is not just how the performers are moving in relation to the camera, but also the choice of location in which it is filmed, the types of lenses used and the accompanying soundtrack: all contribute to shaping the on-screen world of your video dance.

Locations in video dance

The fact that video dance can take dance out of the theatre is a major appeal for artists and audiences alike. Very often, people will remember video dance by the location in which it was filmed. Test this out on yourself: how often do you refer to a work as 'the one set in a . . .'.

Spaces, and how you choose to present them on screen, greatly affect how the viewers interpret what they are seeing.

This is on the level of how the geography or architecture of a particular space impacts on the dancer's movement. It is also because every environment brings with it certain resonances and even quite specific associations.

Given the power of location, it is vital to think carefully when deciding where to film, so that your locations add to, rather than detract from, your completed video dance work.

In many respects, you can't really properly begin to imagine what your video dance is going to look like before you decide in what sort of environment it will be filmed.

How straightforward the choice of location for your video dance is will depend very much on the idea for your work. Some ideas are closely bound up with a particular space or place, whereas others leave more room for interpretation. For example:

- It may be that your idea for your video dance is connected to a very specific location or series of locations, such as the steps of St Paul's Cathedral or inside Grand Central Station.
- It may be that you know the generic type of location that you need, for example, a city park, or a living room, or a dance hall, but you do not have an exact site in mind.
- You may have a more impressionistic notion of what you need, say a long thin space with white walls or an atmosphere that you want to create, or you may want to film in a 'neutral space' – that is, a space that contains the dance, without imposing a particular aesthetic (if that is possible).

These are all valid starting points for working with location that can then be developed and turned into a reality.

Establishing your priorities

Although your choice of where to film will be determined by the idea for your video dance, in many respects your idea also needs to be informed by the type of location you and your collaborators are interested – or willing – to work in. This is because location not only effects what your work communicates, but it also impacts greatly on the way that you can shoot and, most crucially, the dancers' ability to perform.

Let us say, for example, that your idea for your video dance is movement based and that you want to explore the filming of complex choreography that employs lots of jumps and lifts.

If that is the case, then you really have to film in the type of environment that will enable and support that kind of movement. If the dancers need a sprung wooden floor and an interior space to do what is required of them, then this 'restriction' must be incorporated in the idea for your video dance, so that the choice of location is appropriate to the idea as well as the movement vocabulary and the performance expectation.

'It's about finding some fabulous warehouse that has these wonderful design elements that excite everybody, but it's got a concrete floor, and nobody is going to be able to do the movement that has been choreographed because they will just wreck their bones. So what do you do? Well, I've put down a few dance floors in my time and the challenge there is to try and make it look completely natural and part of the location.'

Miranda Melville, production designer

Space, scale and the appropriateness of human movement

The choice of location and type of movement that takes place within it is not just about what is physically possible for the dancers to achieve. It is also important to consider how the location relates to the dancer's performance and how that is experienced by the viewer.

What you really want to avoid is that whoever watches your video dance immediately questions why the on-screen performers are dancing. If they do, it often comes down to the fact that the dancers' actions feel out of place in the space that they are happening. Or, to put it the other way, the choice of location makes the movement seem contrived.

'Often people just take what they are doing in a theatrical environment and go and film that out in a field or next to a swimming pool. It doesn't work because the world that the performer is inhabiting has got nothing to do with the physical world they are in and so there is a disjunction which is unsettling and not at all satisfying.'

David Hinton, director

For some people, the issue is clear-cut: dance can only happen in a space designated for dance – for example, a studio, a stage, a ballroom or a club. It is also sometimes felt that the dance – and where it is located – needs to be justifiable in terms of a narrative; that is, the story of the work explains why the dance is happening in a particular place.

However, if you were to be limited to this approach, then the true creative potential of the medium would be denied you. There are many video dance works in which the location is not the usual place for dance, but in which there is no question about whether it feels right or not.

Whether movement 'works' or not in a particular location can be a lot to do with the scale of the space – or environment – in relation to the human movement. In my experience, when the location features traces of human existence –that is, buildings or objects – then there is more chance that the actions of the performers will relate better to the environment than, say, if it is simply the great outdoors, full of mountains and trees. Moreover, the choice of movement and how that interacts with its environment contributes greatly.

'The location and the dance style have got to work together – unless of course, you don't want them to work together! Doing ballet in point shoes in the middle of a ploughed field is not a very productive thing. But you may decide: "I want to do it in a ploughed field, but I am going to flatten out the ploughed field and put down a sprung dance floor with black plastic on the top and they'll dance on that." That is then saying something totally different. It's what you are trying to say that is so terribly important.'

Bob Lockyer, producer/director

Forgetting the dance

It is often a failure to get to grips with the integration of dance and location that lets video dance down. Frequently, whilst featuring interesting locations, the work seems to lack any really significant choreographic content.

This is because, as we have seen, there can be an incompatibility between much dance movement and filming on location. The solution most often settled for seems to be to simplify the dancer's movement down to the most basic walking, running and gestures. Unfortunately, this does not always lead to the most exciting video dance.

Instead of this, why not try to find ways of using locations that are interesting and appropriate for your idea, whilst at the same time creating video dance that has inventive, exhilarating and beautiful choreographed human movement at its core?

The best way to do this is to make sure that you have plenty of time to create and rehearse the movement in the location that it will be filmed. As we touched on in the previous chapter, the ideal scenario is to develop and rehearse all the choreographic material and framing and movement of the camera in the location in which you are going to shoot. Then there is little excuse for not integrating all the elements of the work.

Unfortunately, video dance productions seldom have enough time or money to support this way of working. However, it is a useful model to have in your head, as you should strive to achieve somewhere near that situation when you work out the schedule for your own video dance production.

'I think that the more traditional dancey films often don't work for me because it seems forced and false to place someone in a location and then get them to do dance movements, when what they need is the context of a stage, i.e. sprung floors, warmth, light. It just looks wrong. When I work in an environment, I will discard anything that looks like "Oh a bit of dance!" because what I am trying to make is movement that seems right and totally apt for the environment.'

Rosemary Lee, choreographer/director

Integrating the space

Another of the great challenges of filming video dance on location is to have the choreography interact with the space, rather than the location simply functioning as a backdrop. Again, there are techniques you can try to integrate the elements.

For example, when you are working in a space, instead of pushing furniture and other props out to the edges in order to give the dancers as much room as possible in which to move, try pulling things into the centre, thereby forcing the choreography and the location together. By having the dancer move around and through, and even touch objects, you will create the feeling that their actions belong in the location.

Likewise, the way you choose to film the material can help to create an integrated look. Looking through the lens, you explore ways in which connections between the dancers and their environment can be supported and enhanced by the choice of framing and camera movement.

'Try to find a space that is big enough to get the camera as far back as you can, as this gives you the most possibilities, whether tracking or using different lenses. If you are in a small space, you are very limited, whereas if you are in a large space, you can make it seem like a small space by the way you chose to frame it.'

Neville Kidd, lighting cameraman

Different lenses and their effect

As we saw in Chapter 2, fundamental to video dance is the relationship between dance and the camera and how movement is captured in the frame. We also saw how the camera's lens alters the perception of space.

But not all lenses work identically and so, when you are beginning to evolve a particular look for your work, it is useful to consider in more detail the specific nature of the various video lenses most commonly used and how these can be used to create very different effects.

The human eye has a very wide field of vision – most of us can see almost 180 degrees of space to the front of us. (Check this by stretching your arms out to the side at shoulder height. Look straight ahead as you slowly bring them together in front of you. Stop when you first see your hands appear. The angle created by your two arms in front of you is your field of vision, and it is usually around 180 degrees.)

A video-camera lens has a narrower field of vision. It is this restricted view that is at the heart of framing and the creative challenge of making images for the screen. It is this difference to the normal human perspective that is one of the main reasons that it is important to look through the lens frequently as you make your work.

There are three basic types of lens, each of which has a different quality.

Standard lens

Whilst the standard lens has a more limited field of view than the human eye (and a wide-angle lens), it offers the most naturalistic perspective on the world, in that its vision is not distorted.

The space that you see through a standard lens looks very much as does it does through your own eyes, with the sense of perspective appearing to be normal and unaffected.

Wide-angle lens

A wide-angle lens frames more of the space in front of the camera than the standard (and telephoto lens), although its field of vision is still usually narrower than that of the human eye. At the same time, it functions rather like a magnifying glass, creating an enlarging effect on anything close-up in the frame.

Some extremely wide-angle lenses, such as, for example, those typically used on a CCTV camera, show even more space than the human eye takes in, and the result is a distinctive 'goldfish bowl' effect.

Even in a more modest wide-angle lens, there will be some distortion, in particular in terms of the perspective. Through the wide-angle lens, the foreground/background relationship of the image appears to be stretched out away from the camera, giving a sense of more space between objects in the frame than there actually is.

This can have a dramatic effect on movement away and towards the camera. Through a wide-angle lens, the dancer appears to travel more quickly, rapidly shifting from far away to very close and vice versa.

In contrast, movement across the frame from left to right, and vice versa, can seem slower, as the wide-angle allows a wider vision than the standard or telephoto lens.

A benefit of filming with a wide-angle lens is that it treats camera movement kindly, seeming to smooth out any minimal bumps and jerks. This can be particularly useful when filming handheld.

Telephoto lens

The telephoto lens works a bit like a telescope. It allows you to frame more distant subjects, appearing to bring them closer.

The telephoto lens creates the effect of squashing the space in front of the camera, making the objects in the frame seem closer together along the line of perspective than they actually are.

A telephoto lens can make movement across the lens seem faster than it is. By narrowing the field of vision, dancers (or parts of dancers) will pass through the frame more rapidly than they would through the frame of a standard or wide-angle lens. This can be very dynamic and often creates wonderful, abstract images.

Most digital video cameras are fitted with a zoom lens, which can usually be moved between standard, wide-angle and telephoto shots. It is only when you want to push the ends of the scale – that is, extremely wide-angle or narrow telephoto shots – that you will need to change lens or use an adaptor attached to your standard lens, if your camera has the facility to do either of these things.

What sort of lens you film your video dance with is a matter of aesthetic choice. Different sections may use different lenses to vary the effect and to communicate different experiences of space and movement.

The best way to learn about the effects of different lenses is to see for yourself. The more time you spend looking through the lens of a camera, the more you will develop an awareness of the characteristics of the different lenses. Soon you will instinctively know which lens to use when you want to create a particular perspective on some movement and its relationship to the space it is in.

On-screen design

As you look through the lens, what do you see? It is a close-up of someone's face, but the lilac wall glimpsed behind reminds you of somewhere that you've been. Is it a flower pattern you see? That blue shirt is nice and shiny. And what is the significance of that chair leant against the wall?

These are the types of questions that will flit through the viewer's head as they watch your video dance . . . and you thought that they would be studying the detail of the dancer's movement! Well, they might be, but they will also be picking up on, and interpreting, everything else in frame.

In the context of making film and video, the term 'production design' refers to the whole look of the work and, whilst incorporating the location, it also includes the on-screen performers' clothes and how they wear their hair and make-up, as well as the colour on the walls and the choice of any object or prop to put into the space.

Design also works on other levels. For example:

- It involves the interplay between shape, colour and texture within each frame.
- It incorporates the way that the choice of lens or the use of light affects the look of everything in shot.
- It takes into account any post-production techniques, such as black and white or colour saturation.

When starting to think about the design of your video dance, the kind of questions you need to ask include:

- Is the work set in a specific time or era that implies a certain décor or look and style of clothing?
- Must the design help to create the effect of a particular environment, such as underwater, or somewhere very hot or cold?

Tip!

The weather and
the elements can
help to shape
your on-screen
world and are an
important design
consideration.
Imaginatively
used smoke and
wind machines,
fans and hoses
can all contribute
to adding texture
and atmosphere.

- Is the idea for your video dance based around a particular object, such as, for example, a sofa or a car?
- What kind of colours and textures do you imagine on screen?
- How can the design help to make a distinction between different sections of the work?
- How can the design help to create the illusion of different spaces being part of the same on-screen world?

Remember that video dance design is not necessarily about creating somewhere that looks like reality. It can just as well be about adding shape, colour and texture into the background or foreground of a shot. It can work in extremes, abstractions or fantasy; it can be minimal or over the top. And to be truly effective, it must always work in conjunction with the lighting, framing and post-production of the work.

In professional productions, the production designer is one of the key creative individuals on the team. They often come from a visual arts background and have the skills necessary to construct, source, paint, disguise or transform everything that appears on screen. Even on a college or workshop project, it is a good idea to ask someone to help with the design of your video dance, as the right person can contribute greatly to the overall look of the work and can also take responsibility for the many practical tasks involved in the design aspects of a production.

Costume considerations

'Our costume designer, Holly, works with us from Day 1. The research that she does in terms of costume is like a dissertation. We were very happy with the red dress in *Motion Control* – it's beautiful. It's covered in body transfers, and when the camera goes in close and allows you to really see it, it's tendon, muscle, it's blood, it's body, it's physical! The work that went to actually achieve that look is absolutely gob-smacking.'

Liz Aggiss, director/choreographer

Part of the overall design of your video dance involves deciding what the performers are going to wear on screen. Like the choice of a location, the clothes worn by a dancer communicates volumes about who they are and what they are doing. This is something that you also need to exploit creatively in your video dance.

The kind of questions you need to ask are:

- Are the performers wearing 'real' clothes' or 'dance' clothes and how does this relate to their on-screen identities?
- What is the colour palette of the costumes, and how does this fit in with the use of colour in the overall design?
- Similarly, what sort of textures and patterns can you work with, and how will these contribute to the image on the screen?
- Will the costumes restrict the dancers' movement, and, if so, how can this be incorporated into the development of the choreography?

If you don't understand the significance of costume and the practicalities involved in sourcing them, it may be tempting just to ask the dancers to find and look after their own costumes. My advice would be to find someone suitable to help you with this important aspect of the production.

As with a production designer, a costume designer can contribute a great deal to the overall look of your work. They may research certain looks and styles and find imaginative ways of enhancing what you are trying to communicate through the shape, colour and textures of the costumes as they appear on screen. A resourceful costume designer may find all the necessary clothes in the dancers' own wardrobes, in cheap or second-hand shops, or they may make some or all of the costumes themselves.

In some situations, a production designer can also be responsible for the costumes. However, it can be that this is too much for one individual and that it is better also to work with a costume designer.

As well as looking at it from an aesthetic point of view, it is incredibly important to take into account the dancer's experience of wearing and moving in a particular costume. As with location, if a costume may potentially restrict or change their ability to perform, then ideally the choreography should be developed wearing costumes.

Similarly, if you are going to expect your dancers to be filmed in extreme conditions – heat, cold, wet – then the costumes need to be appropriate, or you need to have the willingness of the dancers to put up with a certain amount of discomfort agreed in advance.

These boots are made for dancing

Footwear is the single most important aspect of costuming your video dance and is something that should be discussed early on in the process.

What the dancers have on their feet needs to be right for the idea and look of the work, but will also impact enormously on how they perform the choreography. Usually, choreographers prefer the dancers to be wearing the correct shoes right from the start of rehearsals.

Well-chosen footwear can also offer support and protection and can go a long way to making locations with difficult flooring more acceptable and less of a danger for the dancers.

Hair and make-up

As we have seen, in terms of communicating an image, what the dancer is wearing is crucial. Hair and make-up are also part of this and should not be thought of as trivial. Ideally, a lot of your video dance will involve close-up shots of the dancers, and so how they have their hair and the detail of their skin and features will inevitably come under close scrutiny.

As with all elements of production, your approach to hair and make-up will depend on the idea for your video dance.

In some cases, as with the costume, your work may have very specific requirements, because the performer may be playing a specific role or character.

There are some ideas for video dance works that require very elaborate hair and make-up design. For example, you might want to transform the whole look of a dancer into a troll, or a fairy, or some other creature.

On the other hand, often people just want their on-screen performers to 'be themselves'. But you have to know what that means in the context of your video dance and look at the different possibilities and options.

On large-scale film productions, there are usually whole teams of hair and make-up artists. On a video dance shoot, it is often the costume designer who takes responsibility for hair and make-up, or the dancers do it themselves.

What is not an option is to leave thinking about hair and make-up until the day of the shoot – that is just a waste of time and won't necessarily work in your favour. Even if you are expecting the dancers to do their own hair and make-up, you need to have discussed what you want with them beforehand, so that everyone is prepared.

The 'un-designed' work

Some video dance works can be described as being very highly designed, whereas in others the design elements may seem more subtle.

A work that looks like there has been no thought given to design has still been designed, in that by actively seeking to create an 'as we found it' look, or by choosing to do nothing, you are making a design choice.

Similarly, if you find yourself saying 'I just want the dancers to wear ordinary clothes', then you have to think hard about what you mean by that. What is ordinary to you is extraordinary to others: it all depends on the context. What you may mean is that you want your work to reflect your own world and to feel contemporary. You might even want the costumes to be the kind of clothes that you would wear. That is fine. But you need to analyse what exactly that look is and to find out what it contains that is interesting, relevant and unique to your video dance.

Developing the soundtrack

As we saw in Chapter 1, a piece of music or an aural concept can be the starting point of your video dance. But even if it is not the very first idea you have, your soundtrack should definitely not be an afterthought.

Sound is an essential tool that can evoke mood and place and alter on-screen perceptions of space and time as much as the locations, lenses, textures and colours that make up the visual images. That is why,

Tip!

If you want a dancer's hair to look just as they did during rehearsals, you must let them know. You'd be surprised how often someone will book an appointment with the hairdresser the day before a shoot, and in doing so, ruin your plans for their on-screen style.

as you develop your video dance and prepare for the shoot, you need to make important decisions about how you plan to work with sound.

'With *Motion Control*, when I was writing the initial treatment, I wrote the word "hypersound" into the text. The idea for the film had come from the thought, "Why can't it be a dance for the camera in the real, literal, truthful sense of the word?" and I heard the idea at the same time as seeing it. The camera was to be a performer, so it really had to have a sound. Once I'd written the ideas of sound into the treatment and then shown it to Billy, he asked: "What do you mean by hypersound?" And then I could only say it like, "It means iiiiaaaiooooeeiii!" Extremely naturalistic, but with humour and irony embedded within that as well. So it's not just about reality, it's hyper-reality with hyper-absurdity as well. And hyper-extreme imagination!'

Liz Aggiss, director/choreographer

The soundtrack is the name given to everything aural that exists within your video dance. A soundtrack can comprise various elements, including:

*   music – this can be an already existing piece of music or one created specifically for the work, either before filming, or as part of the post-production process
*   actuality sound – this is any sound that is generated by the dancers, or any other animate figures or objects, on screen
*   additional recorded sounds – these can be sourced from anywhere, not just from the on-screen action and incorporated into the many layers of audio that make up the soundtrack.

We will look in more detail at the processes involved in creating a soundtrack in Chapter 10. However, it is no use leaving thinking about sound until that point, as the actual development and filming of your video dance material needs to be informed by your vision of the relationship between sound and picture in your finished work. For that reason, let's now look at some different approaches.

'You need to clear about what you want to do sonically before you film, even storyboarding what you want. You have got to know what you need to achieve and then you can work out how to get it.'

John Cobban, sound designer/dubbing mixer

Music first

Here the choreography of the dancers is created to music, either already existing or especially composed, which is then used as the soundtrack for the video dance.

This approach usually means that the filming and editing maintain the relationship between the dancer's choreographed movement and the music. This in turn often also means that the continuity of the live choreography is also retained.

The major downside of working with music in this way is that it locks you into a particular structure and time frame when editing, which may not work as well in the video dance as it did live.

As we discovered in Chapter 2, this is because our experience of the flow of time differs greatly on screen than in a live context: what can be well paced in the theatre can seem laboured in video. For that reason, the filmed dance often needs to be shortened in the edit and, as a result, the music for the live choreography may end up being too long or have gaps for which there are no appropriate images.

You can get around this problem by asking the composer of the original music to rewrite and record the score specifically for your edited video dance. It seldom works well simply to cut up and restructure the music, although it does happen.

Soundtrack later

The other way to work is to create the soundtrack specifically for the video dance after the filming and when some, if not all, of the editing, is complete.

In this approach, structure of edit is determined by the idea and the nature of the video dance material, and the soundtrack is then designed as a response to this, enhancing and counterpointing the visual images.

This soundtrack may be made up of actuality sounds generated on the shoot or gathered from other sources, or music may be composed especially for the video dance once editing is underway. Often, the soundtrack is a mixture of all these things and more.

Even if it is not going to be used in the final edit, choreographers sometimes choose to work with music when creating the movement. They find that it helps to create atmosphere and to provide energy during rehearsals, and it can also be played as a guide for the dancers on the shoot.

If working this way, be careful that nobody gets too attached to the original music–movement relationship. Sometimes dancers and choreographers can be upset when what they created looks and sounds completely different on screen, even if they have been aware of the process and intention from the outset.

It can be the same in the edit. If you use as a guide a piece of music or sound that is not intended to be part of the final soundtrack, it can be hard to let it go when the final version replaces it.

We explore techniques for using music and recording sound on the shoot in Chapter 7.

'When I created the movement for *Heartthief*, I worked to a piece of music that I really loved. It was very difficult for me to then see the film in the edit without the music that I'd got used to. The movement had really come from the emotion of the original music and now the sound that was being used had a completely different quality. This was one of the very few conflicts I had with Deveril, my co-director.'
Litza Bixler, director/choreographer

Who creates your soundtrack?

Whether it comes early or late in the process, you can choose to have your soundtrack created especially for your video dance or to use an already existing piece of music or track. You may have good reasons for taking the latter approach, however, be warned that if your work is shown beyond a purely educational context, you may end up having to pay either a recording artist or publisher (or both) a lot of money for the right to use the music.

A better – and often more interesting – approach is to have your soundtrack created uniquely for your video dance. Unless it is also your area of expertise, you will probably want collaborate with a composer or a sound designer, or both, depending on the skills and interests of the individuals and what kind of soundtrack you want.

The composer's role in video dance-making is to compose, score and then record original music, which will then be integrated into the sound-track. He or she may ask musicians to play and record the compositions. This music is then usually edited in a computer before becoming part of the overall soundtrack.

Ideally, the composer should be involved from early on in the development process. You need to share with the composer the ideas and inspirations behind your video dance and to discuss thoughts on mood, structure, influences and even the types of sounds and instruments you imagine being used.

Once rehearsals get underway, the composer may visit the studio to watch what is going on and may start to produce material for you and the choreographer and dancers to listen to and perhaps use in rehearsals.

Later on, early samples of music can be used in the edit, as it can be very useful to see how the musical and video images start to work together.

After the edit is complete and the picture is locked (see Chapter 9), the composer needs plenty of time for additional composition and scoring as well as to rehearse and record the final music.

Director and composer should go through the edited video dance together and discuss where and how much music is needed and what it should be like. There may be quite a bit of toing and froing at this time, as it is crucial that the final version of the music for the soundtrack is exactly right.

It can be a good idea for the director – and the choreographer – to go along to the recording, as they can provide moral support and useful feedback on the nuances of the musical performances.

These recorded tracks are then taken into the sound dub and integrated into the overall soundtrack by the sound designer. We look at this stage of the process in greater detail in Chapter 10.

The needs of video dance

In video dance, the roles of composer and soundtrack designer are often blurred, for many composers will actually be responsible for designing and creating the whole soundtrack, and sound designers often also compose original music.

However, there are not necessarily that many people who can success-fully fulfil both roles, and you may well have aesthetic reasons for wanting a composer to compose some original music for your video dance, with a soundtrack designer then creating the overall soundtrack.

Whatever way the work is divided up, the most important thing is that those involved understand the nature of the relationship between sound and image in video dance and, crucially, the fact that the needs of the screen must have priority.

For some composers, writing music for film or video can be an extremely frustrating process and one that, they feel, threatens their artistic integrity. (Sound designers tend not to have the same issues, maybe because the focus of their work is always to create soundtracks, rather than 'stand-alone' music.)

This is because the priorities of the music have changed. It is no longer so important how a piece of music is shaped and formed as an entity in its own right, but rather how it supports and enhances the visual images. In this, the composer and soundtrack designer must be guided by the director, for he or she has the overall vision for the work.

Having said that, the impact of the music on your video dance can, and usually is, enormous. Like in the movies, where in the history of film-making there have been countless instances of composers having their work rejected or, worse still, cut up in the sound dub, there are even more times when the music has defined and immortalised a film or film moment.

The crucial factor is that it must be the needs of the video dance that dictate the nature of the music. Unless you are involved in some conceptual process, in which you want the music to be able to exist in its own right, you must work with a composer – or sound designer – who understands and accepts this enthusiastically. Otherwise, there will be many battles and you may not end up with the soundtrack that you want and need for your video dance.

Exercises

The first exercise in this chapter requires a camera and at least one dancer. For the second, you will need a television or monitor, player and access to existing video dance works or the results of earlier exercises, plus some way of playing music.

Locations on screen

Working in groups of three to five, each write a location down on a piece of paper. It needs to be somewhere that you could literally go to and start filming in: permission is easy to gain; it is not dangerous; it doesn't involve lots of hassle getting to, and so on.

For example, the list might look like this.

- The stairs on the way into the building.
- The main shopping precinct in the town.
- Katrina's kitchen (she lives round the corner).
- The inside of the phone box on the street corner.

Go to each of your locations and spend some time filming.

The choreography does not have to be complex. You can set an improvisation if that feels like a better approach.

Look through the lens of the camera and film as you explore what you are seeing though the lens.

Try out lots of different angles and camera movements. Ask the dancer or dancers to move through and in different parts of the location. Be guided by the space and what it offers. This is not about creating a perfect shot – it is about generating ideas and practising looking!

At the end of the session, look back at the material. Ask yourselves some questions.

- What do you see?
- What does it make you think of or feel?
- What was the space like to dance and film in?
- How does that relate to what you see on screen?

- Do you have the sense of some kind of congruity between the movement, the way the camera is framed and moves and the location?
- If you were to work further in this location, what would you develop?
- Are there things that could be added in that would enhance an idea or look that is suggested by the nature of the location?

The impact of sound

Take a section of video dance, perhaps from one of the earlier exercises or from an already existing work.

Source a variety of different musical tracks to play whilst you watch the video dance (you can do this by simply placing a CD player next to your monitor), or play live musical instruments.

Notice the effect that different music has on the way that the video dance comes across.

CONTENTS

CHAPTER 5

Making Strides

Filming dance usually involves many people, too little (or no) money, difficult environments and tight schedules. Added to this, you are also hoping that magic will happen, for the sole purpose of the shoot is to create the images and performance that will make your video dance unique.

Forward planning and careful preparation of the practical and administrative side of things will help to maximise creativity when it comes to the actual filming. The following chapter contains a lot of advice on the nitty-gritty of pre-production which will help you succeed, whatever the scale of your project.

Devising a plan

Every video dance production needs a plan. That is, it is essential to work out the time frame in which the work will be made, identifying key dates by which certain decisions must be finalised or tasks completed, in order to keep you on schedule for completing your video dance on time and with the greatest success possible.

If you are working in a professional context, time and money are always closely bound together in video dance production. How many days you can rehearse, film and edit for are dependent, to a very great extent, on how much money you can afford to pay out.

Depending on the nature of your production, there are other factors that you may have to take into consideration when devising a production plan.

- Know the date by which your video dance must be totally ready. This may be determined by a first screening or broadcast and is usually called the 'delivery date'. By working back from this date, you can calculate how much time you have in which to complete your video dance.
- If there are any people who are key to your work – for example, a particular dancer or lighting cameraperson – then you need to take into account their availability when drawing up your production plan.
- If your video dance is dependent on a particular season or other environmental factor, again this has to be considered when you are scheduling your shoot.

Even if you are working in a very low-key, no-budget way and there is no externally determined delivery date, it is good to make a production plan. Particularly when everyone is working voluntarily, it is very easy for other things to come in the way and frustrate the completion of your project. Agree a clear timetable with your collaborators at the start and this is less likely to happen.

Similarly, if you are making your video dance as part of a college course or workshop, there will be deadlines by which time you will need to have completed the work. You will have the added challenge of scheduling your production alongside all your other study commitments and most likely there will be constraints on your access to equipment, locations and other students with whom to collaborate. Again, devising a production plan early on in the creative process will help keep you on schedule.

By offering a step-by-step guide to the entire video dance-making process, what you read in this book can help you to make your own production plan. In the Diary section (see p. 225), you can find out about the making of *The Truth* from my perspective as director and co-producer, and this also offers an overview of the process and gives further insight into the multi-layered approach needed to ensure that everything is ready on time.

Working with a producer

In Chapter 1, we explored the collaborative nature of making video dance and saw that the production process often has key creative individuals at its heart. However, one person who has not been mentioned so far is the producer.

According to the Hollywood movie-making model, and to a large extent also in television, it is often a producer who is the driving force behind a production. He or she often works for a independent production company or runs their own. As a choreographer–director team, a choreographer going it alone or indeed any other type of core collaboration, a decision that you will need to make early on in your process is whether you are going to enlist the help of a producer.

To help make this decision, you need to consider the kind of involvement you might expect a producer to have in your process.

Typically, producers play a key role in fund-raising and, once the money is in place, keep on top of the budget and do cost reports. They usually also help to build up the creative team. On smaller projects, where there is no production manager (see below), the producer will do a lot of the organisational work, and on a 'no budget' project, that will be their main role. The producer is also usually very involved in the marketing and distribution of a completed video dance.

A simple way of defining the role of the producer is that, whilst the director is responsible for everything that happens in front of the camera, the producer takes care of everything that happens behind the camera. It is never quite as easy to separate out as that, for, as we will see,

Tip!

Buy a year planner and mark the key dates and deadlines of your production. Put it up on the wall of your production office or studio, where everyone involved in the project can see it.

continually through the process of making video dance, decisions made 'behind the camera' have enormous impact 'in front of the camera'. This is why, if you decide to work with a producer, it is vital that you are sure that they understand your artistic vision and are sympathetic to how you want to work.

A good producer will support you in every way that is possible to achieve your creative vision. They will believe in what you are doing and will use their experience and energy to help you see the project through, from the initial idea to the completed work and beyond.

Even in a college or workshop situation, it is a good idea to have someone take the role of producer. In a 'no-budget' production, there can be more need than ever to have an individual on board who is dedicated to the organisational aspects of the process.

Creating a team

Film and television production has evolved with an almost militaristic approach to hierarchy. What lies underneath is a tried and tested method of working as a team, in which people are hired according to their specialist skills and everyone has very clearly defined 'job descriptions'.

When you are deciding how to make your video dance, there is absolutely no reason that you must base your process on the conventional film and video production model. You – and your collaborators – are free to decide how you want to work.

However, it is useful to consider how responsibilities have traditionally been divided up, not least because it can illuminate the many different aspects of the production that need to be taken care of. If your video dance project is on a smaller scale, involving fewer people than are listed on the following pages, individuals may double up on roles and responsibilities.

The different areas of film and video production, such as camera and lighting, design and office-based production are often referred to as 'departments'. The people who work in the different departments often work in teams. Therefore, if you employ a particular lighting camera-person, you may find that they will want to bring with them their own favourite camera assistant, grip and sparks. Unless you have a really strong reason not to, go with this as these people will be used to working with each other and will hopefully function well as a unit.

People who might be on a shoot and what they do

Director of photography

The **director of photography** (DOP) is responsible for the overall look of a film in terms of how it is lit and shot. He or she will work with the director to decide on which lenses and filters are to be used. He will liaise with the camera operator on the framing of the images and with the spark on which lights are needed. If shooting on film, the DOP decides what sort of stock should be used, according to the expected lighting conditions and the desired aesthetic.

Camera operator

The **camera operator** operates the camera and works closely with the director, the DOP, the choreographer and the grip. He or she is responsible for the framing and movement of each shot.

Lighting cameraperson

On a video shoot, it is usually the case that you will have a **lighting cameraperson**, who both lights the location and operates the camera, rather than a DOP and camera operator. Because of the central role that the camera plays in video dance, it is crucial that you work with a lighting cameraperson who understands and can facilitate your vision with energy and creativity.

Camera assistant

On big film shoots, there are usually two **camera assistants**, who have different, very specific roles.

The **first assistant camera** or **focus puller** stays close to the camera at all times. He or she will usually change the lenses when necessary. Perhaps the most crucial part of their job is that they operate the focus ring on the camera lens. For example, in a moving camera shot, when the focus needs to be changed during the take, they will work out what adjustments need to be made in order to have the focus on the desired part of the frame. It is often said that the focus puller has the most stressful job on set – if they misjudge, a take that might otherwise have been perfect can be ruined.

When working on film, the **second assistant camera**, sometimes also called the **loader clapper**, is responsible for loading the film magazines and for fetching and carrying lenses and other camera equipment as and when needed.

On a video shoot, there is usually only one **camera assistant**. He or she always has lots to do and their speed and efficiency makes an enormous difference to how smoothly a shoot runs. The camera assistant is responsible for helping the lighting cameraperson in any way they need. He or she is in charge of the stock (unused video tapes) and the rushes (tapes with filmed material on), will reload the video camera with tapes and fresh batteries, and set up the monitor. The camera assistant sometimes also doubles up as the grip, setting up the tripod and pushing the camera on a track if needed.

Grip

As we will explore in greater depth in chapter 7, the equipment that is used to support and/or move a camera is called 'grip equipment' and the person who is responsible for operating this equipment is usually referred to as the **grip**.

A skilled grip is a crucial member of the creative team. If you imagine, for example, that you wish to film a shot that combines a circular tracking movement with a particular movement by the dancers, then you will realise the importance of the grip's input.

It will be his or her skill, judgement and ability to recognise choreography and move steadily and sometimes even in time to music, that will be the key to the success of any take. In fact, in this sort of situation, the camera operator relies on the grip to carry out his or her job well, for they only have control over the camera lens and not the actual movement or timing of the camera through space.

On complicated moving-camera shots, you will often find that it works best when the grip and the dancers talk directly to each other to sort out any problems to do with the speed or positioning of the camera in relation to the dancers' movement.

Spark or gaffer

The **spark** or **gaffer** are the names given to the specialist film or video lighting electrician who will rig any lights that you need in your location. They work closely with the DOP or lighting cameraperson and advise on what are the most suitable lights for a particular effect or location. Sparks often work for or run companies that can supply the lights that you need (and often also special-effects equipment such as smoke and dry-ice machines).

Sound recordist

The **sound recordist** is responsible for recording any audio you need from your shoot. He or she will usually also operate any musical playback that is needed on location.

On big productions, there is often need for an **assistant sound recordist**. The most usual role for this person is to operate the 'boom', which is a long pole with a microphone attached. This job requires good judgement (and strong arms), as the microphone is usually held above the action and moves with it to retain a consistent sound level and quality. If there is no boom operator, then the sound recordist must do this job.

Assistant director

An **assistant director** can be a real life-saver for a director. There are so many things to think about during filming that having someone to help run the shoot can make a big difference.

As well as contributing to scheduling, a good assistant director will take care of much of the logistics and timekeeping, leaving the director to focus on directing the performers and the camera.

On large-scale shoots, there can often be three assistant directors, who each have a very specific role. The **first assistant** will be in charge and he or she will also ensure that the shoot stays on schedule. The **second assistant** traditionally makes sure that the performers are all on set and ready for filming when they are needed. The **third assistant** is on the move, often acting as a satellite to the first assistant, stopping pedestrians from passing through shot and waiting with equipment. Assistant directors always have their walkie-talkies on.

Runner or gofer

The **runner** or **gofer** is the person, as the title suggests, who has to run off and fetch things when needed. An efficient, resourceful and reliable person in this role contributes massively to the success of a shoot.

The role of runner or gofer is often the one that aspiring film- and video-makers find themselves in when they are trying to gain experience. The downside of this is that, of all the people on the shoot, the runner often sees less of the actual filming process, as they are always being sent off to do things away from the action.

Location scout

Finding the right locations for your filming is an essential, yet can be a time-consuming part of the video dance-making process. If a production calls for a great many locations, a **location scout** can ease the load by doing the initial search for suitable places in which to film.

Location manager

The **location manager** is responsible for everything to do with the different locations – for example, obtaining the necessary permissions, organising parking and ensuring that the place is returned to its original state when filming is completed.

Production manager

The **production manager** is responsible for the co-ordination and administration of the project, in terms of booking crews and facilities and creating and distributing schedules. They work closely with the producer and director on all aspects of the production.

Production designer

As we saw in Chapter 4, the **production designer** is responsible for the look of everything that appears in shot.

Costume designer

Likewise, the **costume designer** has a responsibility for what the on-screen performers wear. This can involve making, gathering and buying clothes and shoes. On smaller productions, the costume designer will also help the performers to dress for each scene and will take care of the costumes on the shoot.

Hair and make-up

On really big shoots there are often teams of **hairdressers** and **make-up artists**. On smaller shoots, one person will often do the performers' hair and make-up, or they do their own, depending what is required.

Other people who may be involved in your video dance

Editor

The **off-line editor** takes the filmed material and shapes it into the final work. The **on-line editor** then creates the final master version of this edited work. His or her responsibility is mainly to ensure any required technical specifications are met and will also often add graphics, titles and special effects in the on-line edit.

Colourist

A **colourist** operates specialist picture-grading equipment with which he or she will make any necessary alterations to the colour of each frame of the edited video dance.

Composer

The **composer** writes the original music that is to be used in the production. He or she will works closely with the director and together they will work out what is needed for the video dance. As we explore in other chapters, the music can be written at different stages of the process, depending on how you want to work.

Soundtrack designer

The **soundtrack designer** creates the soundtrack of the video dance. He or she may also be the composer or may incorporate music by another composer into the overall audio design of the work.

Dubbing mixer

The **dubbing mixer** creates the final soundtrack by placing and mixing all the different audio elements including music, 'actuality' sound (see p. 149) and added effects. He or she is also responsible for laying down the final version of the soundtrack onto the master tape.

'If I'm going to work with somebody, I'm often attracted to people whose aesthetic is somewhat my own, and yet somewhat foreign and fascinating.'

Laura Taler, choreographer/director

Selecting the right people to collaborate with you behind the camera is as important as finding the right dancers to perform on screen. There is no limit to artistic and practical input that a highly skilled and creative individual can contribute to the work. Conversely, the wrong person can do untold damage with a bad attitude or a lack of care. So choose carefully.

In a college or workshop situation, there may be students who are interested in particular areas of production and who can offer valuable creative contribution. Identify them and ask them to take on a specialised role in the team, but be sure that they understand the nature of the commitment and exactly what their responsibilities will be.

When you are working on a larger scale or professional production and you are looking for collaborators, there are a number of approaches that you can take to gather together a creative team.

- Watch and listen to other artists' work. If you like the way that something has been costumed, filmed or edited, or think the soundtrack is great, then check out the credits to find out who is responsible.
- Go on personal recommendations from other practising video dance artists.
- Advertising in local film and video workshops, or trade magazines, or through an on-line resource such as www.videodance.org.uk can be a good way of making contact with new people to work with.

You will probably recruit people to work on your production at different stages in the process. That is to say, there are certain people who need to be onboard from the very beginning or early on in the process – for example, the director, choreographer, production designer, producer and composer. Other peoples' involvement – the lighting cameraperson, the sound recordist, the editor – may be confirmed at a later date, once you are clear about the timescale of your production and when exactly you are planning to film and edit.

'Directing is difficult but it's not rocket science. The hard stuff is to make a team out of very, very different people. It is the people-skills side of it that is so important. That can mean anything: you take them out for a drink, or have a chat quietly in the corner. You don't have to be a nice guy the whole time. You can also be tough, but you have to be tough and be smart, smile and know what you are doing, because they can smell you a mile off, the guy who doesn't know what he's doing.'

Ross MacGibbon, director

Who's behind the camera?

A crucial question that often arises when deciding what sort of team you want to work with is whether you should operate the camera as well as direct, or whether it is better to work with a cameraperson.

As always, there are pros and cons in either scenario.

- If you have little or no experience of video, or if you find that the thought of operating the camera fills you with terror, or you show no talent for it whatsoever, then stick to working with a cameraperson.
- On the other hand, the digital cameras that many of us use in our video dance projects are relatively easy to operate and can give super results, from a technical point of view at least. This should give you the confidence to both direct and film your own work, if that is what you want to do.

'In the beginning, when I was making films with Merce Cunningham, I was also the cinematographer, but as the work developed, I needed to stop, because I saw him being distanced from the entire process. I would be on the floor with the dancers and telling them what to do and making the work. And he would be sitting at the table and getting impatient. So that's when I started to hire camera people, and I would sit at the table with him, we would discuss the ideas and we would make notes together about what was being filmed.'

Elliot Caplan, director

Some reasons to operate the camera yourself:

- You don't have to communicate exactly what you want to see in the frame to anyone else.
- You can respond freely to what you are seeing as you film.
- Unless the cameraperson is able to be in rehearsal a great deal of the time (and this is usually dependant on budget), as the director, and maybe even choreographer of the work, you will be more familiar with the movement material.
- Operating the camera yourself can save money, in that you do not have to hire a cameraperson for the shoot.
- Without a cameraperson, there is one less person in the space, which can matter when the location is tiny.

Some reasons to work with a camera operator:

- An experienced cameraperson will bring a wealth of knowledge and creativity to your production, not least because in most video shoots, the camera operator will also light your shoot. Lighting for video is a whole new area to learn about (we look at the basics in Chapter 7).
- As the director, having someone else behind the camera enables you to remain one step removed from the filming process. If you are not the one with your eye pressed to the viewfinder, but rather can stand back and see what is actually happening in space, it can be easier to find solutions to problems that arise in the filming.
- If you are operating the camera, you will find that you effectively disappear behind the camera lens. This can leave your collaborators – dancers, choreographer, designer and so on – feeling rather abandoned.

Finally, if you are already both directing and choreographing, shooting your video dance as well may be one responsibility too many, and it is better by far to spend some time and energy finding the right camera-person to work with.

However, choose your cameraperson carefully, for their impact on your video dance is enormous. As well as being technically and aesthetically adept, they must be:

- happy to move with the camera, whether this is handheld or on a track
- interested in the processes of the dancers' performance
- willing to try out ideas, even if they are unusual and appear to break film or video conventions
- fit and energetic, and keen to look, listen and share ideas.

'Alkin Emirali, the camera person who shot *Anarchic Variations*, was fantastic. It's very weird camera work, in many ways, and we were asking him to do some very bizarre things. But he is very creative, and he's also a big tai chi person, and so the physicalisation of his role became a really important part of the process for us all. From a performer's point of view, that was great, because he was responding in the moment, like another performer. It is important to find the person who can do what you need without getting in a bad mood or saying "This can't be done!", "No, I don't do this." '

Liz Aggiss, director/choreographer

Your choice of camera

Related to the question of who will shoot your video dance is the issue of what sort of camera to use. This book is not the place to go into lots of detail about the various makes and models of cameras available. You must do that research yourself. Often, camera-hire companies, shops and professional camera people can give you the best advice on the most up-to-date equipment. It is worth noting that most technology you can buy in the shops becomes obsolete – or at least very dated – after three or four years.

There are, however, a few general principles involved in deciding what sort of camera to use that may be useful to explore here.

We are talking about digital video cameras and the market is divided into three levels: professional, semi-professional and domestic. The main difference between these is price.

A professional video camera costs so much money that most people who use them hire them on a day-by-day basis. Only if you were a lighting cameraperson who is frequently in employment would you possibly consider buying one.

Domestic – or consumer – cameras are the ones that many people now own and use to record holidays, family life and celebrations.

In the middle price range are the semi-professional video cameras. A lot of broadcast television is now shot on these cameras, and they are affordable to smaller production companies, video workshops, universities and colleges, and even artists who receive commissions.

Of course, the cost of the cameras is not the only factor, but it is true to say that, the more you pay, the better the quality of the visual and audio recording will be. This is down to two things: the quality of the lens, and the ability to have as much control as possible over the image.

Lenses

The quality of any video image is largely determined by the lens. Again, the more money that is spent on the lens, the better.

A good (i.e. expensive) lens will give you a crystal-clear image, full of depth and will cope brilliantly with colour and lack of light. A cheap lens will not.

It makes sense then that the lens on a domestic camera cannot compete with that on a professional or even semi-professional camera. Nevertheless, many of the so-called 'low-end' cameras still have reasonable quality lenses that can create amazingly good images.

Controls

Making video dance requires the creative use of the video medium. Part of this is having control over such factors as the focus and exposure of the images that you shoot.

Most cameras have auto settings for many of the functions that you or your cameraperson may in fact want to decide on yourself, according to the specific aesthetic of your work. It is therefore essential that any camera you choose should also give you the option of operating manually. Unfortunately, whilst nearly all cameras do allow you to 'over-ride' the auto setting, their design sometimes makes this and the operation of the various controls rather tricky.

'With the small cameras, Mr Sony is often in the way. He's exposing for you, he's focusing for you, or if he's not, you are struggling to focus, because all the controls on the camera are so small and fiddly and out of the way. So there's a barrier between you and your art, created by the manufacturer. If you can break that down and keep everything manual, then you can begin to get fantastic results.'

Neville Kidd, lighting cameraman

Widescreen

Another factor to look out for is the so-called widescreen capability of a camera.

As we saw in Chapter 2, the video frame is a rectangle.

However, the actual ratio of the top and bottom to the sides of this rectangle is rather variable. For many, the most 'cinematic' and aesthetically pleasing ratio is 16 : 9, which is often described as 'widescreen'. But, for a long time, television was filmed in 4 : 3 and most domestic video cameras still shoot this ratio.

There can be the option to select a widescreen setting within the menu set-up of domestic or consumer video cameras. Be warned that this may not be 'true' widescreen; rather the camera may simply be distorting the image to make it fit into the widescreen dimensions. This degrades the picture quality significantly.

Many semi-professional and all professional cameras shoot true widescreen 16 : 9 dimensions, which is also referred to as 'anamorphic'. In most parts of the world, television programmes must now all be filmed in – and are broadcast – at the true 16 : 9 ratio.

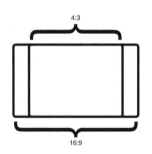

Figure 5.1
The contrast between a 4 : 3 frame and 16 : 9 'widescreen' frame

Format

Related to the sort of camera you work with is the question of format. Even within digital video, there will be various versions available on the market at any given time.

As with the cameras, different formats tend to be graded according to some notion of professional versus domestic, or consumer, quality, some being deemed to be 'broadcast quality' and others not. But, as many of you will be aware, these distinctions can be rather blurred and are, in any case, constantly evolving.

When deciding what sort of format to work with, you have the choice to go with the one that is most easily accessible to you, or to look around and see what else is out there and how it fits in with your vision for your work and the context in which it will be made and screened.

How much money? Budgeting your video dance

Unless you are making your video dance within the context of a college course or workshop, you may need to raise money to pay for the costs of creating the work. There are many different ways to fund making video dance, ranging from applying to specific commissioning schemes run by broadcasters or arts-funding bodies, to using your own money, or raising in-kind support, where companies and individuals give their time or equipment for free. Very often, video dance work results from the combination of all these scenarios.

Calculating how much money you actually need to make a particular video dance – or 'budgeting' your project – is about assessing a number of varying factors, all of which have so-called 'cost implications'. As always, there are questions that you need to ask.

- How many dancers are you envisaging working with?
- Who else will be involved? For example, will you commission an original soundtrack from a composer (often cheaper and much better than 'buying in' already existing music), or work with a choreographer, or cameraperson and a designer?

- What sort of locations do you want to film in, and do they require you and your production team to travel across the world?
- What sort of quality of image do you want?
- What sort of approach do you want to take to the development, filming and editing of the work?

When you are devising a budget for your video dance project at the very beginning of the process, there is a balance to be struck between having a vision of a particular look, quality and approach to working, and what you believe that you will be able to raise.

Much of what is covered in this book can help you to understand and make judgements about these important issues.

Devising a budget

In film and video production, it is usually the producer who is responsible for managing the budget. However, they must always work closely with the director, for how the money on a production is spent is closely bound up with the creative process of making the work.

That is to say, decisions that a director makes about any aspect of the process must be done with an awareness of the cost implications of that choice. Likewise, the producer must collaborate with the director to ensure that money being spent is optimising their creative vision of the work, as well as the artistic potential and welfare of those working on the production.

No matter how big or small, the process of making a budget is the same: you need to work out what it is that you want to do and how much it will cost.

It is then a case of adding, subtracting, shifting and cutting figures and totals, until you have reached the desired amount (that you either have or are aiming to raise).

There are various film- and video-budgeting packages that you can buy, or download, for your home computer. These detail all the different elements of the production. All you need to do is add in the actual figure costs based on your local market prices, and the software will work out your totals, with added lines for things like contingency and so on.

The way I do it is to think my way through the entire production, working out who and what will need to be paid for.

Things that are easy to be overlooked, but should invariably be budgeted for, are insurance, production fees, location costs such as heating, tape transfers and contingency (this allows for any over-spend and is usually put at 10 per cent of the overall budget).

When you are devising a budget at the start of the project, you will be working back and forth between the estimated cost of what you want to do and the estimated cost of what you hope to raise (or have already secured). This means that, whilst you may start of with six days of filming and twenty days of off-line editing, if this brings the budget in above what you have (or think you can raise), then you may have to reduce this to five days of filming and eighteen days of editing.

As with all aspects of the creative process, you need to be clear about your priorities when devising the budget. For example, if a certain location is absolutely essential to your video dance, then you need to find out how much it costs and factor this in as a definite in your calculations.

On the other hand, you may very well not know how much you are going to need for location hire until later, when you have found the locations that you want. In that case, all you can do is make an educated guess at how much to put in the budget under the 'location hire' heading.

Cost reports

One of the essential things to understand about any budget is that it is not set in stone; whilst the limit of your budget is usually capped, how much is actually spent on the different areas can and should be fluid.

This means that, for example, you may have initially budgeted a significant amount for lighting, only to find that the idea develops in such a way that all the filming is going to happen outside in the daylight. Great! You've saved all that money, which is a relief, as you then find out that you had greatly under-estimated the cost of travel and accommodation for the crew and performers over the shoot.

As long as the overall budget does not go over, and as long as no aspect of the production is expected to suffer because another is being over-supported, then a budget can and will change many times in the course of a production.

The way to keep on top of these constant changes is by doing regular 'cost reports'. These are updates on the budget, incorporating the actual spend of every aspect of the production, as opposed to the estimate, which is what the initial budget will have been based on.

Some funding schemes ask to see at least one cost report submitted during the course of the production (sometimes this, as well as a written progress report, is a condition of the next stage of the funding being paid).

Whether a requirement or not, these constant checks on the budget are essential to ensure that you are not going to run out of money before your video dance is complete, and before everyone and everything has been paid for.

Production meetings

A successful video dance production depends to a large extent on a shared vision. Whilst as director, you will meet and discuss various aspects of the production with individual members of the team, it is also a good idea to have regular production meetings, involving the key personnel. This would normally be the choreographer, lighting cameraperson, designer, producer, production manager, and possibly the composer.

Here, information can be shared, ideas and opinions expressed and the team spirit nurtured. Just make sure that these production meetings are well run, held somewhere comfortable with tea and biscuits on tap, and that they don't happen too often. There is nothing more wasteful and frustrating than attending an unnecessary meeting.

Finding your locations: some practical ideas

Finding the locations for your video dance involves a great deal of looking and asking around, lateral thinking, following up false trails and persever-ance. Rest assured, however, that this work pays off, as the choices you make will have a major impact on the finished video dance.

The production designer, who is responsible for the look of everything in your video dance, can be a great collaborator on this job, and he or she may already know many of the film-friendly locations available in your area.

On my own productions, I like to do a lot of the location hunting myself. This is because the starting point of my work tends to be a formal or emotional theme and so the nature of the location or locations is often very open to interpretation.

I find that it really benefits the overall creative process for me to go and look at many different possible locations, as this helps to narrow down the feel and look of the video dance that I am developing. If there is a production designer working on the project, then visiting different locations together can be a great way of developing a shared vision for the overall look of the video dance.

There are a number of stages involved in finding the location or locations for your video dance.

- Clarify the nature and role of location in your video dance.
- Decide on the geographical area within which it would be feasible for you to film. There can be a trade-off between the cost and hassle of transport and accommodation for cast and crew and finding the perfect location at the right budget.
- Research and find specific locations that appear to fulfil your remit.
- Go to look at these locations and assess their suitability from an aesthetic and practical point of view. You may find yourself back at the researching stage many times before the hunt is over.

Tip!

If you are struggling to find the right location, ask other artists if they have any recommendations and check out if there is a local screen location bureau or similar resource that you can access.

'I could bring the director to a location because I like one particular aspect of it and then he or she might look at it from another view completely. It is a useful way of progressing the collaboration and the work.'

Miranda Melville, production designer

Recceing your location

Going to look at potential locations in which to film is often called 'scouting'. You will probably 'scout' a great deal of locations before finding one – or a few – that seem to fit the description of what you are looking for and are worth pursuing further.

Once you have found some places that you think may fulfil your needs, then you need to 'recce' them. 'Recce' comes from the military term to 'reconnoitre': to survey or inspect (an enemy's position [*Collins' Dictionary*]). In video dance-making terms, recceing involves visiting the location and looking (and listening) from both an aesthetic and practical point of view.

There are many different types of information that you may need to ascertain when you are recceing. Again, you may need to return to the location a number of times, each time focusing on finding out different types of information, until you are sure that it is the right place for your filming. As you can see, if there are a few different locations needed for your video dance, the work really starts to mount up. It is essential to build this into your production plan, as the shoot can't go ahead without somewhere to film.

It can also be very helpful to take others with you. As we have seen, the production designer is often actively involved in the initial choice of location. Given the impact it has on both the making and outcome of your work, it's wise to include your collaborating choreographer in the choice of locations.

Tips for successful recces

If at all possible, recce a location at the time of day, or night, on the same day of the week that you plan to shoot.

You might, for example, visit a quiet back street on a Wednesday afternoon and decide that it is perfect for your needs, only to turn up to film on a Saturday morning to find that there is a market in full swing.

Similarly, a location can look very different at different times of the year, depending on whether the trees have leaves on them or not, or other similar seasonal changes.

Take photos or shoot video footage at each location. My personal preference is for photographs, as I like to have prints to lay out in front of my collaborators as we discuss locations, and to put them up on the wall.

Before you start, draw up a checklist of all the things you need to know about a location. Your considerations need to be a mixture of the aesthetic and the practical and, in the end, the decision where to film will often be a balance between the two.

The very first things to find out about a location are

1. Is it available when you need it?
2. If it costs money to use a location (and it often does), do you have any or enough money to pay for it?

Now, there may be flexibility on both your side and the side of the person with the location as regards these two issues. Managing video dance budgets is very much about weighing one cost up against another. So, for example, whilst your perfect location may be more expensive than you had budgeted for, it may save you money on accommodation and transport because of where it is. This means that you can afford to spend a bit more than you had planned, without going over budget. Obviously, if you are working in a no-budget scenario, then you'll have to persuade whoever owns the location to let you use it for nothing.

As regards the question of availability on certain dates, you can refer to your production plan to discover how much room to manoeuvre there is in your schedule.

Having established these facts and knowing that filming at a particular location is a real possibility, the next questions to ask about possible locations should include those listed below.

- To what extent does this location represent what you imagined?
- What is it that interests you about this location?
- What do you want to see of this location through the lens?
- How much additional work would you need to do to create the exact environment you need for your video dance? This work might include clearing and cleaning, painting and decorating and set-dressing – for example, bringing in furnishings and other objects.

Tip!

Be sure that the person giving you permission to film in a particular location actually has the authority to do so.

- If there are windows or skylights in an interior space, how will these affect the lighting of your shoot? Will they be featured in shot, form part of the overall lighting, or would they need to be (and could they be) blacked out?
- What physical features does the location have that will impact on the choreography and performance of dance? As we have seen, the main issue is usually the floor.
- Is there enough room to work? Remember, not only do the dancers have to perform, but you also have to fit in a camera (which may also need to move), lights, grip equipment and essential crew, at the very least.
- What will the camera see of the location as it moves around? How much of the space can be featured and how much would you have to hide or dress? Are there some angles from which you would not want to film and how would such a restriction impact on your filming style?
- If you know that you want to film a tracking shot that will feature all 360 degrees of the space, are there places in which lights can be hidden? Often, the solution can be to hang the lights from the ceiling. Is that possible in this location?
- If you plan to record sound, is it feasible to make the space totally quiet? Or are you happy to also record the ambient sounds of the location and incorporate these into your soundtrack? Alternatively, is the location so perfect visually that you are willing to work around any sound problems, with the awareness that this may put a strain on your post-production budget?

As well as these mainly aesthetic questions, there are many practical issues to consider about each location.

- Is there access to electricity on the location? If possible, recce potential locations with your lighting cameraperson and even the 'spark' (shoot electrician). They will check out the power supply in the location and, if it is not adequate for what you require, can advise on hiring a generator. This is a cost that then needs to be factored into the expense of using a particular location.
- How will you heat the space? Is there suitable heating already in the location that you can use and, if so, what will the charge be? If there is no heating, where will you source space heaters and how much

will they cost? Also, will the power supply support heating as well as lights? If not, again you may have to hire in a generator, or gas heaters.

- How will your creative team travel to and from the location?
- How will you transport the equipment there?
- Is there parking? Can you pre-book the parking in order to secure it? You don't want to waste time on the shoot days looking for spaces for all the vehicles (you need to work out how many there will be on each day of filming). If there is not parking in the vicinity, can people and equipment be dropped off and the vehicles left elsewhere? Who will do this?
- Apart from the actual spaces in the location in which you want to film, what other facilities does it have? For example, is there a space where the performers can warm up and rest during filming?
- Is there somewhere that food can be prepared and served? Alternatively, are there suitable places serving food nearby, and will your budget stretch to taking everyone out for lunch and maybe also breakfast and dinner if required?
- If the actual space in which you plan to film is very small, are there other rooms nearby in which cast and crew members who are not involved in a particular scene can wait in relative comfort?
- Is there a secure place where additional equipment can be stored during the shoot and possibly even overnight?
- If you need to place lights outside the location – for example, shining through a window – where can these be placed, who needs to be informed and what safety measures need to be carried out? If you are leaving a light on a pavement or any other public space, you will need someone from the production team guarding it at all times.
- If the location is a public space, what impact does this have on your filming and how will you minimise any disruption to the public?
- Will you need to seek permission from anyone appearing in shot? How will you let the public know that you are filming?
- Will you need to – and be allowed to – cordon off certain areas?
- What other measures will you have to take to ensure that there is no conflict between your needs and the rights of the public?
- Do you need to inform the police or other authorities when and where you plan to film?

Many of these practical questions may seem far removed from the creative process, but in video dance-making, like all film and video production, working out the practicalities to this level of detail is completely bound up with the artistic vision.

As the director, you do not necessarily need to find out all this information yourself. Your producer and production manager, if you have one, as well as the production designer, can all help out with this important part of the pre-production process.

Once you have the answers to all these questions – and there may be others, depending on the specific nature of your idea – then you can make a realistic judgement as to whether a particular location is the right one for you to film in or not.

Whilst your choice should be based primarily on aesthetic considerations, the impact of all the practicalities, especially on your budget if you have one, must also play a part in the decision-making process.

The illusion of locations

When you are thinking about the type of locations that you need, it is important to understand that the actual geography of your video dance – that is, how all the spaces featured fit together – is something that can be created through carefully planned filming and editing.

This means that you do not have to find one location that fulfils every architectural or spatial requirement of your work. Instead, you can film in different locations and, through framing and editing, achieve the illusion that they are interlinked.

For example, if you have a shot of a performer disappearing through a door in the side of a building followed by a scene within that building, there is nothing to say that the interior space has to be – in 'real' life – the interior of the building that has the door on the side of the wall.

Similarly, interconnecting interior spaces do not all have to be part of the same location. To work effectively, however, such illusions must be carefully planned, as the screen space must make sense to the viewer. As we will see later on in this chapter, the design elements, as well as the storyboarding of your video dance, can play an important role in getting this right.

Filming schedules

As we saw at the start of this chapter, your production plan gives you an overview of the process of making your video dance. However, when it comes to the filming days (and those directly leading up to them), you also need to make detailed filming schedule.

The purpose of this schedule is to let everyone who is needed on the shoot know where they must be, at what time, on every day. Importantly, it also helps you to work out how much time you have to film all the different sections of the video dance and it lets your collaborators know what material is going to be filmed when.

When you are setting out to devise your shooting schedule, the information that you need includes:

*   how much and what material you plan to film
*   how many days you can film for and how long these days will be (there are guidelines, usually issued by the unions, on how many hours a crew can work within a set period of time)
*   how long it will take to set up (prepare the locations, rehearse the dancers and camera, set up lights and equipment) and to film the different sections of material
*   how much preparation can be done in advance, and what must be done on the day.

As we saw at the end of Chapter 3, the process of working out what you want to film is one of gradual clarification, which should end up in some kind of storyboarding or shot list. This process will help you know what you are hoping to film and how complex each set-up or scene will be. This can also be a great help in working out how much time you will need.

Devising the shooting schedule is the director's job, for he or she has the responsibility of ensuring that what is needed is filmed in the time available. However, it is best done in collaboration with all the key per-sonnel on the project, as their experience and knowledge of the different aspects of the filming process will be invaluable in making up a realistic schedule.

For example:

- the lighting camera person can estimate how long it might take to light a particular location or scene
- the production designer can let you know how long is needed to dress the location on the day (much of the work will ideally be done on the days leading up to filming, if access to the location is possible)
- the dancers can give you an idea of how much time they need to warm up before filming
- the producer will keep you clear on how many filming days there are and other factors that will impact on the schedule.

Learning how to gather everyone's information and how to make a realistic estimate of how your time should be planned is something that comes with experience.

When devising a schedule for your shoot, you have to make sure that you allow enough time to carry out what you want to achieve, otherwise you may have to end up compromising your work by having to miss out sections or by having to hurry through them. On the other hand, there is no point in being too pessimistic, as aiming to film too little doesn't help to create the sense of urgency often needed to encourage a drive in the creative team. It will also mean that you don't end up filming as much material as you could have done. It's always good to have lots of options in the edit.

As we will see in the next chapter, once filming begins, schedules can, and often do, go awry for all sorts of unavoidable reasons. But making an intelligent and well-thought-through plan for each day will go a long way towards optimising what you can achieve from your shoot.

Your shooting schedule should include the following information.

- Details of everyone working on the shoot, i.e. name, role and mobile telephone number.
- Detailed directions on how to reach the filming location, either by car or public transport, including maps and where to park on arrival.
- The time at which people are to arrive and be ready to work. (This may vary for different members of the team depending on their involvement.)

- What you are planning to shoot when and how much time is to be spent setting up, rehearsing and then filming each section or scene.
- Break times for meals (usually an hour) and for tea (15 minutes), and details of the catering arrangements.
- Details of dressing and warm-up rooms, equipment storage and any security information.
- Any necessary travel times and information if you are changing locations during the course of the filming day.
- Any environmental factors or special features that need be taken into account. For example, if you are filming on a beach, what are the times of high and low tide and what are you aiming to capture?
- Any other information that you consider important for everyone working on the shoot to know in advance, for example, anything to do with their health and safety.

The build-up to a shoot depends on good teamwork, under clear leadership. You will find that decisions need to be made quickly and often. You are depending on your team to help you get everything ready on time and to give you feedback on any issues that come up.

Crucial aspects of your video production can be overlooked through lack of communication and through assuming that someone has taken care of something when they have not. As director, you should never make assumptions. Instead, talk to your team and make sure that everything has been done to your satisfaction. Devising the shooting schedule is often the best way of ensuring that every aspect of the production has been carefully thought about and prepared.

You have to think through and take measures to ensure that the practical aspects of the process enable your artistic vision. Be aware that every decision made will impact on the way that your video dance turns out in the end.

Not taking good care of your crew and performers is the biggest mistake you can make. No matter how inventive your ideas, you as director depend on the creative abilities and goodwill of many people, and they in return need and deserve to be given what they require in order to do their jobs to the best of their abilities.

For example, it might seem trivial to be thinking in detail about where and how your creative team is going to have lunch, but if you don't make

Tip!

Have a few spare copies of the schedule for anyone who loses theirs during the course of the shoot.

plans for this – and make sure that they are the best plans in terms of ensuring that people are well fed, in a manner efficient in time and effort – you will find that you waste valuable shooting time, which means that you might end up not achieving everything that you need.

Your final schedule should be completed a few days before filming commences and distributed to everyone who is working on the production. If your work is funded, the commissioners or executive producers like to have a copy of the filming schedule for reference. They may also want to visit the location whilst you are filming. If you know this in advance, it can be a good idea to make a note of this visit on the schedule, so that everyone else knows too.

This detailed preparation of a filming schedule will lay the foundations for a successful shoot and will offer you the best possible chance to achieve your goals. A clear plan also allows for greater flexibility in the face of everything being different. On a film or video shoot, things will inevitably crop up that you cannot have anticipated, but if you are well organised and have a clear vision of what you are setting out to achieve, this will not be a problem.

Exercise

Practical recces

- Return to the locations that you filmed in as part of the location exercise in the previous chapter. This time, go without a camera.
- Before you set off, make a list of the kinds of practical questions you would need to resolve if planning a shoot there.
- When finished, decide whether this would be a suitable location for filming, both from a practical and aesthetic point of view.

CONTENTS

CHAPTER 6

When the Shoot Comes

When the first day of filming arrives, there is more than ever to think about. Over the next two chapters, we look in some detail at what happens on the shoot and how, as director, you will simultaneously be dealing with the practical, the aesthetic, the psychological and the emotional. Let's start off by considering the shoot as a performance.

The shoot as performance

The shoot is where your vision for your video dance really starts to become reality. Whatever you have imagined, sketched out, discussed and rehearsed is all leading up to this point.

This is when your attitude will make an enormous difference. Remaining focused, calm and alert is essential. Even if you have worked out exactly what you want to film each day and in which order, when it comes to actually having everyone assembled in one place and working together, things can become unpredictable and time, concentration and energy can easily slip away.

But equally, what happens on the shoot can – and often does – exceed your expectations. The moment of performance, when camera and dancers come together on location, looking great and giving their best, is an extremely exciting event. Enjoy the experience. And make the most of it, by keeping you imagination alive and working actively with the material as it unfolds in front of you.

Who runs the shoot?

Even though video dance is usually the result of the collaboration between different artists, when it comes to the shoot, it is essential that there is one person 'in charge'.

As we have seen, even the simplest filming requires considerable organisation, energy and money to make it happen. It involves dancers and crews working closely together. It may involve being on location, lighting and much other technical equipment. All these things have to be co-ordinated and, on top of all this, everyone's performances need to be their very best ever.

The way to ensure that the shoot is as successful as possible is to have everyone understand what they need to do and when. And this requires one person to be leading from the front: the director.

This does not mean, however, that nobody else on the shoot has input. On the contrary, it is important to find ways of working that make the most of the many different skills and talents of the production team.

A wise director knows that the advice of an experienced lighting cameraperson, sound recordist or production designer should never be ignored.

If a choreographer and director are collaborating, when it comes to the shoot, the choreographer will often focus on the well-being and performances of the dancers, allowing the director to concentrate on guiding the camera crew and making sure that all the other aspects of the shoot are running smoothly.

However, all this does not detract from the fact that the director must have the final say on what needs to be achieved and how it will be done, and this must be respected and supported by everyone. It is the only way that filming can be carried out as efficiently and harmoniously as possible, and the results will show in the final video dance.

Dealing with what you are seeing

Even if you have expended a great deal of energy visualising what this might look like, you will find that everything changes when the imagined becomes reality on the shoot. The space you are working in and how it is lit, as well as the quality of the camera lens and what the dancers are wearing all impact enormously on what you see through the viewfinder.

In many productions, the shoot day will be the first time the dancers and cameraperson are together in the filming location. It is also often the case that any rehearsal filming has been done on a different, usually less expensive, camera than the one that is being used on the shoot. Again, this will make a big difference to how the material that you have planned actually comes across.

Unfortunately, as we have seen, video dance budgets and schedules rarely stretch to having rehearsal time on location, with everything and everyone in place. In my experience, you might not even have had the chance to work with the cameraperson in the rehearsal studio, as time and money are so short and people's availability very hard to co-ordinate.

This situation is far from ideal. However, by knowing exactly what you want to achieve artistically, being fully prepared from a practical point of view and with the support of a good team, you can overcome these difficult aspects of the process. As we saw at the end of Chapter

3, a well-thought-through storyboard can provide invaluable guidance, helping you to work out how much has to be filmed and reminding you of the creative vision that you and your collaborators have planned for.

'Sometimes when I am preparing a shoot, I forget how long things take to do. Often, the bigger the production becomes, the slower things get. On the *Death and the Maiden* shoot, there were scenes where I'd hoped we'd have lots of detail and close-ups. For a scene that was around two minutes long, I'd plan for ten or twelve shots, but in the end we only had time to film three different shots. That was really painful. I'd watch the rushes and say: "This is beautiful, but it's not the way I pictured it."'

Laura Taler, choreographer/director

The shape of the filming day

Tip!

Because they usually come from such different professional worlds, it is easy for the camera crew and the dancers to feel shy of each other. Make sure that your team are introduced when they first start work. It really helps people to work if they know everyone's first name.

Being organised in your approach to each filming session will give you the best chance to achieve what you want, efficiently, safely and with maximum creativity from all involved.

Every day of every shoot of every video dance production has a completely different nature, but there are certain basic procedures for filming that are useful to use whatever the situation. Here are some ideas for ways in which to structure your time.

At the beginning of each new day, or new filming session, start by looking at the scene or section of material that you want to shoot first.

Ask the dancers to perform in the space in which you are planning to film this particular material. As many of the creative and technical personnel should be present and watching as possible. To work efficiently as a team on the shoot, it is important that everyone has a good understanding of what is happening. At the very least, the lighting cameraperson, production designer and sound recordist must see this early run-through, but it is generally better if everyone there focuses on the dancers for the short time that it takes to watch through the material.

The dancers perform, or mark through if they are not warm, the material that is to be filmed first and, as the director, you can now explain what it is that you want to see through the lens and how you think this will be achieved.

The lighting cameraperson, spark, production designer, sound recordist and so on will be looking and listening to the run-through with slightly different agendas. Some conversations about logistics will follow, and people may need things clarified.

At this point, you can use your storyboard to help you explain what you imagine being framed in each shot.

Now it is time for to make the final preparations before filming begins.

- The dancers will continue to warm-up and put on costumes and make-up.
- If this is the first time that the dancers have been in the location, they will also need time in the space, with the choreographer, to work out how to perform their movement in this new environment.
- The lighting cameraperson will work with the spark and his assistants to set the lights and with the grip to put in place any tracks and other equipment required.
- The production designer will make final alterations to the location, according to your description of the shots that you are planning to film next and what parts of the space will be seen through the lens.
- The sound recordist will be setting up microphones or, if his or her work is done, may start to help the camera crew set up.
- Runners will generally be helping out.

At this point, the director sometimes finds him- or herself with nothing to do. Relax and enjoy the experience. Use the time to gather your thoughts and to check your notes and storyboard, for within a minute or two someone will come up and ask you a question and the moment will be gone.

It is important that everyone knows at what time you plan to start filming, or to 'turn over', as it is often described. When you are drawing up the daily schedule, you should have made a realistic estimation of how long it will take everyone to prepare for each different scene or set-up. As things progress, however, you may have to reassess the schedule, for things are always different on the day.

Once people have seen the walk-through of what is to be filmed next, it is a good idea to check if your planned time to turn over is feasible, now that they know exactly what they are up against. But also be aware of how this fits into your original schedule for the day and try not to let things drift too far. Encourage people to work as swiftly as they can by making sure that they have the information and help they need to carry out their responsibilities.

Communication between everyone is vital on a shoot. This is often where a good assistant director can be a real asset, as he or she can help to organise the many different things that need to be happening simultaneously and to keep things moving.

Setting a shot

The moment on the shoot when everyone is ready to film is an exciting one. There is an air of expectancy and always a certain tension, with everyone geared up for the first shot of a new work, day or scene.

If you did a walk-through of the choreography you are planning to film, as described earlier, it is now that the team reconvenes, their set-up work complete, ready to start filming.

When everyone is together again, remind them what it is that you want the dancers and the camera to do.

The type of direction that you give to the camera operator will depend on your chosen method of filming.

- You can describe, verbally and using a storyboard, the specific shot that will capture an entire section of movement – for example, a low-angle wide shot of Anna's solo.
- You can explain what it is that you are interested in seeing in the lens – for example, 'Keep Jane's head in frame as she performs a duet with Anna' – allowing the shot to alter continuously as the sequence develops.
- You can take a more spatially oriented approach, setting up a physical relationship between the dancers and the camera and asking the camera operator to frame the parts of the choreography that come into shot. For example, you could film a duet by laying a circular track,

set the camera to the desired height and frame size, then ask the dancers to perform inside the space created by the track. A continuously evolving shot is then captured by having the camera circle round the dancers as they perform the duet.

Ways of developing the choreography of the dancers and camera are discussed in Chapter 3.

Ready to go

Once everyone is clear about what they are doing, it is time for some rehearsal and then to 'go for a take'.

If this first shot involves camera movement, start by doing a 'stagger' – that is, ask the camera and the dancers to move through the action at half speed (or less). That way, you can check that everyone knows where they are going and help to avoid collisions.

Depending on the nature of the choreography, it may be difficult for the dancers to perform slowly, but they can always mark the movement – that is, trace the shape of the movement, without doing anything extreme, like lifts or jumps – until everyone knows exactly where they are going.

Rehearse the sequence through a few times until you sense that the most obvious pitfalls have been discovered (for example, lights coming into shot, dancers not having enough space, camera operator not understanding what you want to see in frame). Once these types of issues have been ironed out, it is time to shoot the first take.

When you are working out the logistics of how to achieve a particular shot, it is often best to let the dancers, cameraperson and grip, if there is one, talk to each other directly. The dancers are the ones who know the choreography best and, if they understand what you are trying to achieve, they will often find the best and simplest solutions.

'As the camera operator, if you don't talk to the dancers and make a connection, it shows on camera. If you get to know them, have a laugh and a chat, they also want to give something to you, not only to the director and I think that comes across in their performance. They may not think about it, but if you have a relationship, then they generally like you and you all become part of a team, working together and for each other, under the guidance of the director.'

Neville Kidd, lighting cameraman

How much rehearsal?

Tip!

Do not start your filming day with the most difficult shot. Allow people to settle in and the team to gel by filming some of the easier sections first.

Knowing how much rehearsal you need before going for a take is a matter of experience and judgement. What you want to avoid is rehearsing until everything is perfect, then going for a take, only to find that everyone has grown weary and concentration is lapsing. Often, the best approach is to start filming quickly, even whilst people are still feeling the way a bit.

In these days of relatively cheap digital video, there's actually nothing wrong with shooting every rehearsal. In fact, you will probably find moments of useful material even within these first takes. The downside of this approach is that you can end up with hours and hours of material, which you will find a real chore to look through at the editing stage and in the midst of which it will be easy to lose the really excellent moments!

The solution is to find a happy medium between giving everyone some practice, yet being brave enough to start filming whilst the material is still a bit raw and edgy.

Calling 'Action!'

There are some well-known conventions for what to say when you want to start and stop filming. It is usually the director who calls 'Action!' and 'Cut!' and, if this is a new role, you may feel a bit self-conscious yelling out these familiar words. Get over it: your team needs clear direction and that starts with knowing when the filming of a take is to start and to stop.

'Action!' is the standard command for a shot to begin, whereas 'Cut!' means that the action should stop and the camera and sound should cease recording. But things can be a bit more involved than this.

It is important to realise that neither camera nor dancers can go instantaneously from waiting to begin, to the moment that you want a shot to begin.

It's best to give people warning that things are getting going. So, with everyone in position, start the whole process of a take by calling out 'Stand by everyone. Prepare for a take!'.

Then, still before you instruct 'Action!', you will need to cue the camera to start filming. No matter what the technology, the camera must be recording before the shot begins. It is too late to press the record button on 'Action!'. From when you ask the camera to 'turn over' (the term often used for 'start recording'), wait to hear back from the cameraperson that they are ready and recording (the term often used in 'speed' or 'rolling').

It is now time to cue the dancers' action. Like the camera, the dancers can't usually go from a stand-still to performance instantaneously. You may have to cue them to start moving, and then call 'action' for the camera when they have reached the point (in the movement and/or in space) from where your planned shot is to be filmed.

There may be other elements of the shot that also need cueing. For example, if the dancers are performing to music, then this will need to be playing for them to start dancing. There might also be special effects, such as smoke or wind machines that need to be cued in time for them to take effect in the shot.

The cueing of a scene needs to be worked out carefully and rehearsed, and this can only be done on the actual shoot, when everyone is together in the location. It is important, however, to allow plenty of time in the shooting schedule for all this fiddly work.

If the cueing of a scene is very complicated, an assistant director can be a great help. He or she can start off the different elements in the right sequence, leaving the director to call 'Action!' when everything and everybody are as they should be.

Finally, think about how you call 'Cut!'. If the dancers are mid-way through an intense performance of a section of choreography, don't just shout 'Cut!' (especially if they are in mid-air!).

It is more sensitive to wait until a phrase is completed or, especially if they are improvising and you don't really know where things are heading, warn them that you want to stop filming, for example, by asking them to 'draw their dancing to a close', before then asking the camera to cut.

Tip!

If using music on the shoot, it is vital that the dancers, choreographer and whoever is operating the music playback should identify key cue points that can be located quickly. Valuable filming time can be lost as a CD or tape is spooled through to find the right bit in the music.

Setting the tone

As the director, I feel it is my role to set the tone of a shoot. If I am well prepared and present myself as confident and considerate, purposeful and polite, then I gain and maintain the respect of those I am working with and they will feel able to give the best they can.

But I also try to allow others to be themselves and to have some laughs as we work, as people invariably work better when they are relaxed and feel like a team. However, the director also has the responsibility of making sure that what is needed is achieved, and becoming too laid back or distracted can lead to time being wasted and people becoming frustrated and losing concentration. If this happens, not only might you fail to get the material you need, but even more seriously, accidents occur when concentration lapses.

Crunch points come when you have been struggling with a particularly hard shot or section of filming. Once it is achieved and you all feel relieved, it is important to have a few moments of relaxation.

Unless it is planned, however, you have to make sure that these moments do not become impromptu 'tea breaks' because before you know it, you will have fallen way behind schedule.

This is where you have to be sensitive, yet alert. People need to recover after a period of intense concentration but, as the director of the shoot, you also need to hold on to your wider goal and keep things moving along.

If you start to fall behind right at the beginning of filming, you will feel under pressure all day. This is a good reason to make sure that your schedule is realistic in the first place. Don't panic though if things seem to go awry early on because, if you manage to stay focused and you are able to keep things on course, time can right itself and suddenly you will find that you have achieved what you wanted and you are back on course.

If you are running behind, do not be tempted to delay or, even worse, abandon scheduled breaks without first consulting your team. Not only would this be extremely inconsiderate, it can be very counterproductive, as people always work better when they have had the chance to recuperate over a cup of tea or something to eat.

If you do need to run over slightly, let's say by 15 minutes, in order to finish off a scene, make sure that everyone knows and agrees to this (including those who are waiting to serve a meal or hot drinks). Do not just put your head down and keep going; you are much more likely to gain your team's co-operation if you involve them in your thoughts and gain their consent.

This also goes for the end of the day. It is not good practice to keep on shooting beyond the scheduled end of the day. The way to avoid this is to plan a realistic schedule in the first place and to keep on top of your timekeeping throughout the day.

Nevertheless, sometimes things do take longer than expected and so, if you really do need to work late, again make sure that people agree to this. Don't just spring the idea on them at the time when they were meant to be finished. Rather, gather everyone together as soon as possible and ask them if it is OK continue for, say, an extra hour?

If they agree, this gives them the chance to let anyone who needs to know that they are going to be finishing late. If you are making changes to the plans, make sure those working away from the set, such as costume, make-up and those in the production office, are also consulted and kept informed.

It is also is crucial that you keep the dancers informed of any changes in the schedule, both in terms of altering times and the order in which you are planning to film the material. They need this information to help them to mentally and physically prepare and to manage their energy through the day.

'Good directors make you feel wanted and enabled. Bad directors make you feel like they are the only ones that have done anything and you are just there to serve them.'

Ross MacGibbon, director

The dancer's experience

'It's very challenging for performers to work in film because, often, you're having to repeat the same bit again and again. I think it boils down to whether, as a performer, you're a sprinter or a long-distance runner. If you're very good at dancing in small bursts, then film is fine. If you're better over a long period of

time, then I imagine film can be very, very frustrating. Some people are good at negotiating both, and I'm always impressed by people who can perform very well in film, but also very well on stage.'

Litza Bixler, director/choreographer

Amidst the complexity and excitement of working with a crew and camera, location and lights, it is easy to overlook the fact that the most important people on the shoot are the dancers.

The shoot is performance time. It is now that the dancers will be creating the emotion, character, shape and energy that will be at the heart of your completed video dance and, ultimately, how they perform on camera will determine the success of your work.

Dancers are both athletes and artists. Unlike actors, whose movement for the camera is most likely to be fairly pedestrian, dancers are required to use their bodies in a much more extreme way. Even the simplest choreography becomes physically challenging when it is performed on location and repeated many times.

For the majority of dancers, their experience will have been of performing live in a theatre, which has a very different requirement in terms of how energy is used. They will usually have one (or perhaps two) shows per day and their daily routine will be geared towards being ready to perform in one energetic burst, lasting anything from a few minutes to a couple of hours.

In contrast, on a video dance shoot, a dancer must be ready to move all day and will be asked to perform for much shorter chunks of time, over and over again. Inevitably, filming involves a lot of waiting around, as lighting and other technical aspects of the production are worked on. This can be extremely difficult for a dancer, who not only has to keep his or her body warm but must also keep the focus of the performance alive.

'The challenge is how to remain physically warm and mobile during the shoot, because there are gaps and pauses and you have to hang around a lot.'

Karin Fisher-Potisk, dancer

Dancers have needs, both practical and artistic, and these should be uppermost in your mind, not only during the planning of the production, but also throughout filming. This way you can feel confident that they are able to give their best and work through the specific challenges of making video dance.

Start by considering the all-important practical needs of your dancers.

Don't expect the dancers to arrive first thing in the morning and be ready to dance in front of the camera within a short space of time. No matter how minimal the choreography, in order to perform well and safely, dancers need plenty of time to warm up their bodies. When you are planning your schedule, it is a good idea to consult the dancers as to how long they think they will need to prepare to move. Remember that this is time for them and should be in addition to what they will require to put on costumes and do hair and make-up. Be aware that the dancers will also need warm-up time after a major break, such as lunch.

Dancers really appreciate and benefit from having a space of their own, in which they can warm-up and rest in between sections of filming. If possible, find a space well away from the noise and chaos of setting up the lights, camera equipment and the last-minute dressing of the location. Make this place as warm and as comfortable as possible. If necessary, put mats or bits of carpet on the floor. Bring in some ballet barres, mirrors and some comfy chairs, cushions or beanbags. Again, it is a good idea to ask the dancers what they would like.

Filming on location can be a very cold experience and, whilst those behind the camera can layer up with fleeces and puffy jackets, dancers' costumes rarely seem to provide the necessary insulation. This is a problem, as it is not only difficult, but also dangerous for dancers to perform when their bodies are cold.

There is not much that you can do about the outside temperature, other than only film during the summer and even then, for many of us, that does not guarantee warmth. But you can take measures to lessen the impact on the dancers. For example:

- Make sure that the costumes the dancers are wearing are as warm as the visual aesthetic allows, by using thick materials and, where possible, providing thermal underwear.

- Have warm overclothes, blankets, drinks and hot-water bottles standing by for the dancers to use the minute they finish a take.
- If you are filming inside, make sure that you can use any heating available and organise that this is on early enough to heat the space before the dancers arrive. If there is no heating in place in the location, then you must consider hiring space heaters, which come in various sizes, depending on the scale of the space you need to heat. This is something that must be budgeted for.

In order to keep their energy levels high, dancers need to eat and drink often, and you should make sure that there are snacks and water available for them all the time. Check beforehand what they like to eat whilst they are working.

Remember, the quality of their work depends on their bodies and minds being well fuelled. Regular and properly organised meal breaks are as important to the dancers as they are to the rest of the crew.

On-screen performance

Helping the dancers to perform well on camera is not just a matter of taking care of the practicalities. You must also think carefully about the kind of direction you will give them in terms of on-screen performance.

For example, you need to let them know how you want them to relate to the camera. Should they:

- dance as though the camera is not there?
- imply that they are aware of it, by looking down the lens?

Although subtle in terms of physical movement, whether or not a dancer makes eye contact with the viewer through the lens has an enormous effect on what your video dance communicates.

Depending on how it is done and its context in the video dance, the dancer's gaze might be, for example:

- confrontational
- seductive

- questioning
- playful.

Looking into the camera empowers the dancer, as he or she breaks out of the role of the observed to become the observer. It is always a strong image, and you need to consider carefully when and how you use it.

Avoiding eye contact with the camera does not mean that the dancer and camera (or viewer) do not interact. As we explored in Chapters 2 and 3, through close-up shots and camera movement, the viewer can be drawn closely into the dancer's kinesphere, creating the feeling that the two are involved in an intimate, albeit virtual duet.

The performer's perspective

'When I'm performing our own work, in a way I don't need to be directed. I know where the camera should be. I know how the camera is framing me and I know what I need to be doing. I'm used to thinking about that in terms of directing myself on stage. For me, it's like a live event anyway, performing in front of a camera.'

Liz Aggiss, director/choreographer

Another aspect of directing the dancers that you must consider is how much you want them to know about the particular shot that you are filming. People feel very differently about this, and it depends very much on the look and feel of the work that you are creating.

You may believe, for example, that it is very important that a dancer knows exactly what the camera is framing, so that they can shape their movement and performance accordingly.

You may equally believe that the dancer needs to be clear about the intention of their movement, but that to know exactly how the camera is framing their action at any given moment would potentially affect the dancer's performance in a way that you don't want.

'When filming *The Truth*, I did not know exactly what and how I was being framed by the camera as I danced, and this was probably a good thing! It would probably have freaked me out to know how close up my face was being seen, and it would have made me more self-conscious in my performance.'

Karin Fisher-Potisk, dancer

Performing for video dance is a very different experience to performing on stage. Through camera, editing and sound, the shape, quality and emotional and physical impact of a dancer's performance is radically altered. Whilst the dancers remain physically distanced from the audience, their performance is central to the nature of the work and what it communicates on screen.

This seems to be a situation that dancers either like or don't like. In my own experience, dancers have always been excited by the new possibilities offered by video dance and go into the creative process with open hearts and minds. However, there have been times when a dancer has watched footage of their performance on the shoot and they've been disappointed, feeling that what they experienced as they danced was far more intense that what they see on the monitor.

However, more often the opposite has happened and when a dancer has seen, for example, an extreme close-up of their eye as they perform a slow movement or, after editing, through the effect of the repetition and looping of certain of their movements, they witness that their performance has risen onto a whole new level of intensity, very different to what is possible on the live stage.

'My performance always works better on film, 'cos I'm not a big performer, and as a dancer on stage, I always did quite small things, such as eye movements that didn't register with the audience. I love the fact that in film you can make use of those little intimate moments. But, at the same time that you can be physically smaller on screen, as a performer you also have to be energetically bigger. Film strips away the energy of your performance so that, when you are in front of the camera, you have to emanate even more of that energy. But not spatially. It's not about big gestures, but about the energy being more intense.'

Litza Bixler, director/choreographer

Giving feedback

Finally, always remember, no matter how taxing it feels to be the director and/or choreographer of a video dance, it is much more difficult to be the on-screen performer. It is the dancer's every movement that is being scrutinised and judged, and this can be hard to take.

Be sensitive and involve the dancers in what is happening on the shoot. Communicate with them clearly and, most importantly, at the end of a take, always give them praise and thanks.

If you decide to go for another try of a shot, always let the dancers know the reasons. If they were great, but there was an unwanted wobble in the camera work, tell them exactly that. Likewise, if there was an aspect of the dancer's performance that was not right, give them that information and they can try and do better (depending on your particular set-up, it may be the director or the choreographer that gives the dancers these notes).

'I felt that the emotional build of the performance was my responsibility, as it would be on stage but with the added benefit of someone – i.e. the director – being there to let me know if it was not quite right.'

Karin Fisher-Potisk, dancer

Another important thing to think about is the manner in which you give direction, both to the dancers and to the rest of the team. It can feel awkward to ask – or tell – people what to do, or to change the way that they are doing things, but as director, that is your role.

Don't be mealy mouthed and become unclear in an attempt to avoid telling people what you want. Be clear and direct, but also be polite and say 'please' and 'thank you' as often as you can.

Working with a monitor

A monitor is a television screen that has an output from the camera and shows you what is being seen through the camera lens and recorded onto tape.

A monitor can be useful on a shoot for the following reasons.

- Through it, you can see exactly what is being filmed. This helps in terms of being able to feedback to the team and it can give you the confidence that you are getting what you need for the edit.
- Other members of the creative team can use it to check aspects of their work on screen. For example, the cameraperson might look at it to check the effect of a certain light or the designer might look at it to see how a particular colour on the wall covering comes across on camera.

However, there are downsides of working with a monitor. These include, for example:

- Because they are heavy to carry, monitors often encourage you to keep the camera in one position. This can mean that you not exploiting the full potential of the moving camera in video dance.
- If you sit with head down, eyes glued to the monitor screen as the filming takes place, you cannot see how the dancers and camera are relating to each other in space. This can make it hard to work out why a particular shot is not working.
- A monitor can also create a barrier between the dancers and the technical team. It can be extremely intimidating for the performer in front of the camera to look up and see everyone crowded round looking at the monitor. As the monitor usually has to be positioned well out of the way of the action, this can also create a very remote feeling for the performers.

Whilst I like to have a monitor on the shoot, I also make sure that I don't become obsessed by it. When I am confident that the dancers and camera operator understand what we are aiming for in a particular shot, I often move away from the screen to watch the performance of a take through my own eyes.

Positioning myself as close beside the camera as possible, I can gain a good idea of what the lens is taking in. By coming out from behind the monitor, I am right there with the dancers and cameraperson, seeing what they are experiencing in a very direct way.

If you take this approach as the shot is rehearsed and then filmed, you can always alternate between being next to the camera and watching the monitor. This lets you refine the shot, whilst still remaining in contact with what is happening 'on the floor'.

'I remember on the *greenman* shoot, being ticked off, that I wasn't giving Simon Whitehead enough praise and direction. Instead, I'd retreated, huddled behind the monitor. I was quite shocked because I pride myself on the relationship I have with the performer, and I felt I was giving him some space. But maybe they were right, that I'd disappeared into the film-production juggernaut, and what they were trying to say was: "Come out, and keep doing what you do best." It's a tough split role one has in that situation, attending to the live or the image.'

Rosemary Lee, choreographer/director

Reviewing on the shoot

The monitor can also be used for on-location reviewing. By rewinding the tape in the camera, you can watch material that has just been shot.

This can be helpful if you are unsure how well a take actually went (even though you may have been watching the monitor, you can sometimes feel that you missed something).

When there is a lot going on within a shot and if there is lots of cueing required in the course of the shot, it can be hard to concentrate, as you may also have to be thinking about, or even looking at, things that are happening outside the frame.

If the choreographer is away from the monitor, or in a different position than the camera, he or she may wish to watch back a take on the monitor, as will a choreographer who is also performing.

If a shot involves the camera moving around 360 degrees of space, it can be easier for everyone, including the director, to get well out of the way and let the dancers and camera operator get on with it. When both feel that they may have achieved a good take, this can be reviewed on the monitor to make sure that you do indeed have what you need.

Rewinding to watch what has just been filmed should not be done too frequently, as it has its dangers.

- The tape can be damaged by being rewound and played in the camera.
- It is also surprisingly easy to forget to take the tape back to the very point that filming finished and, as a result, the next shot that is filmed can be mistakenly recorded over what has just been shot.
- Stopping everyone in their tracks as you review can seriously disrupt the flow of the shoot and expend a great deal of time, with people waiting around and losing focus and dancers growing cold, particularly if watching is followed by a long discussion.

Make sure that you only look back at a take if it is really necessary. It can be better to work out ways in which everyone who needs and wants to can see the monitor during filming, or better still, develop enough trust and decisiveness amongst the core collaborators.

'Sometimes I will say to the choreographer: "That shot was great. How was it for you?" But then it's not good for them and you have this dialogue and I'll say: "Time is getting on. If we do this again, we'll leave less time for the next shot, but can you live with the fact that her leg was a bit bent, because it was perfect for the camera and we might never get the cameraperson to do that move so well again?" The choreographer will maybe say, "No, I really, really have to have that leg straight", and so you go for it again. Or vice versa, she will say, "Wow, that was great!" and I'll say "Well, I am sure the camera could do it better".'

Ross MacGibbon, director

Listening to others and knowing your mind

One of the most crucial times to have clear direction is when you are deciding if you have what you need and that it is time to move onto the next shot or set-up.

If you are well prepared, then you will have drawn up a storyboard or written a shot list detailing everything that you want to film, and, ultimately, all you need to do is to follow that plan.

However, things never work out exactly as you think they will and, whilst it may be better or worse than you hoped for, it is unlikely that the material will be exactly as you imagined it, nor will you necessarily achieve everything that you set out to.

Nevertheless, at some point, you must move on, or you may end up with too much of one scene or section and not enough of another. Making a decision on this is one of the hardest, yet most important of the director's responsibilities.

The input of others here can be useful, but also potentially dangerous! Remember that it is you who is going to be in the edit suite, putting the video dance together with the editor, and therefore you need to take responsibility for ensuring that you have filmed what you need and want.

You are also the person with the clearest vision of what you are trying to achieve and the timescale in which you must do it. This is where your personal judgement comes in and, above all, it is important to go with your instincts, no matter what anyone else is saying.

However, it is sensible to take on board the points of view of the other members of the creative team. For example:

- Even if a take may have gone perfectly from the perspective of the camera and lighting, the dancers or choreographer may feel unhappy about a certain aspect of their performance. It is important to listen to this and to judge accordingly.
- The camera person, grip, costume or set designer or sound recordist will also all have opinions about how well a take went for them and they will invariably let you know these. Again, all this information can be useful, but ultimately you need to decide when you have what you need and it is time to move on.

Listen to what your team members are saying, look at what you have and bear in mind that there may often be some pay-off between the perfect camera movement and best performance.

You can decide to go again and retake the shot, but remember that, if by doing this you are going to fall behind schedule, you may lose out completely on something else later on. Moreover, going again will mean that everyone has to recharge their energy, and there is a point at which performance – of camera and dancers – will be at an optimum and from that point on, things may not improve. There is a balance that must be reached and, to a large extent, this judgement is at the heart of directing.

Tip!

If you can avoid it, don't watch your rushes at the end of a long day of filming. You are likely to be very tired and even stressed, and you may end up feeling depressed and disheartened by what you see. Leave the material for a few days or even weeks before watching it with a view to editing. You'll be surprised how good it all looks to your fresh eyes!

Be reassured that, as we will see in Chapters 8 and 9, when you are editing you can use any of the material you have filmed, even fragments of takes that you thought were a total disaster on the shoot.

In the edit, in many ways, you can start afresh. You have the material that was filmed in front of you and it is up to the creative vision and skill of everyone involved in post-production to make it into a video dance you can all be proud of and excited by.

CONTENTS

CHAPTER 7

Light and Sound
on the Shoot

At every stage of the video dance-making process, you should strive for the highest possible production values, which means that everything that appears on screen must have been designed, chosen or made to the best possible standard.

When it comes to the shoot, an understanding of lighting, knowing how best to move the camera and to get the best sound recording will contribute massively to the overall quality of your video dance, thereby enhancing the viewer's experience of your work and what it is communicating.

Some approaches to lighting

Lighting plays as crucial a role in your video dance as the choreography of the dancers and the framing, design and editing.

It can also feel like one of the more scary aspects of the production process, both from the point of view of knowing what you want and how to describe and get it, and of having to deal with heavy, hot, fragile lamps on the shoot.

Whatever sort of camera you are using, a great deal of the on-screen quality actually comes from how what is in the frame is lit and how the image is exposed (how much light is allowed into the lens), rather than the format on which it is shot.

This is where the skills of a talented lighting cameraperson can really make a difference to a production, as he or she will be able to help you exploit the creative potential of lighting for video.

However, if you are operating the camera yourself, an alternative is to employ a spark or gaffer, who can also help you to achieve the look that you want. Or learn to light for video yourself, taking guidance from the suggestions below, and with the possibility of doing some more in-depth research, either in some of the many specialist film and video lighting books or web sites, or by attending a workshop in lighting for video.

Another good option, especially if you are part of a college course or workshop, where access to specialist lighting equipment may be limited, is to use the light that you find in the locations that you are filming, the 'available light', as it is sometimes called.

In fact, there has been a whole tradition of video-making that has eschewed the notion of adding in any lighting, working instead simply with what is found on location, either interior or exterior. This can be a really interesting creative challenge and one which you might choose to follow, if it fits in with your interests and personal aesthetic.

The biggest lamp of all

The sun is the biggest and most efficient lamp you can get. Whether you choose to work with special video lighting or not, you need to consider whether you are going to harness the powerful effect of the sun.

If you are filming in an exterior location, then the sun will invariably be part of your look. However, it also remains entirely beyond your control. It can be shining brightly one moment and disappear behind dark clouds the next, changing the whole look of the shot completely. Filming on days when the weather is much duller, because there is an overall layer of cloud, can be easier than on very sunny days.

Big-budget productions sometime use extremely powerful lights that can compensate in the times when the sun's brightness fades, but it is unlikely that you will be working to that scale of production. However, the chances are that you are not necessarily depending on an absolutely consistent look throughout your video dance, and so it may be that the changeability of the sun will simply add texture and movement to your images, rather than spoil them.

A bright sun overhead can also create deep, dark shadows, which may not be what you want. Again, electric lights can be used to 'fill' these with light, and thereby soften them. Sometimes white polystyrene boards or circles of reflective material are sufficient to bounce the sun's light and banish any harsh shadows, but this is not really a viable solution when the subject of the shot or the camera itself is in motion.

Any filming involving the sun is best in the early or later parts of the day. Depending on where you are in the world, there will be a varying window of time in which the sun will be rising or setting, and its rays will be at more of an angle and less harsh than when it is overhead around midday. This can create very beautiful lighting, with gentle shadows, which will greatly enhance your on-screen images. It is definitely worth factoring this into your schedule if you can.

Interior lighting

The sun can still be your most important source of light when you are filming indoors. Many spaces have windows or skylights and deciding if you are going to leave them as they are – and therefore work with the sun – or black them out, so that no sunlight can seep in, is an important decision to make when you are preparing to shoot a scene in a particular location.

As with the exterior location, the benefit of using the sunlight is its powerfulness. However, as we have seen, it can also be inconsistent.

'Daylight is a wonderful light and if you have got one source of daylight coming into a room, then that is fantastic. When you are lighting for the camera, you are always trying to source one main – or key – light. The human eye likes to see the contrasts that are created by one powerful light: it is something that we are used to, we are used to having one sun. So, if you can light with one source, then that is very aesthetically pleasing.'

Neville Kidd, lighting cameraman

If you do decide to black out the sun from your location, or if the space that you are filming in has no windows to the outside, then you need to create everything from scratch.

It is a good idea to work from the premise of no lights, adding in what is needed. Rather than setting up lots of lights in your location then moving them around and trying to work out how to light a particular set-up, begin by looking at the scene in front of you; consider what sort of look you want to create; and then gradually add one light at a time, scrutinising closely the effect of each one.

Working with light

Whether filming outside or inside, working with the sun or lighting everything yourself, the aesthetic considerations are the same. It is the interplay between light and dark that shapes the image in your frame. For example:

- You can have a scene in which there is lots of light everywhere, with small areas of shadow (for example, as if outside on a sunny day).
- Or, a scene might be almost entirely dark, with small areas of light (for example an interior scene, lit by one window or lamp).
- The lighting in some situations can be much flatter, or more 'diffuse', (for example, outside on a dull or misty day, or inside, where the lighting is more general, such as in a shopping mall).

It is important to realise that, when lighting for video, what you see through the viewfinder or on the monitor is what you get. Nothing magical happens as the images are recorded onto tape and so you must strive to be happy with the lighting as it appears in front of you on the shoot.

Having the ability to open up or close down the iris in the camera's lens allows you to control the exposure of the image. It is therefore a creative decision whether you expose for the dark or the lighter areas of each image. In general, however, a predominantly under-exposed video picture just looks dull, whereas one with small areas of over-exposure can be very beautiful.

The biggest challenge when using lamps for lighting for video dance is that the performers, and often also the camera, will usually be moving through the space.

This means that it can be very difficult to find somewhere to place the lights, where they won't come into shot, where there will be no danger that a dancer might trip over or crash into them (remember, these lights are extremely hot and heavy), and yet where they can actually create the desired effect on screen.

The best solution can be to position the lights up above the action, but unless you are shooting in a film studio or theatre, it is unlikely that there will be handy bars in place above the space from which you can hang the lights. This is something you must take into account when choosing your location. Look to see if there is anywhere up high that the lights can be put, safely out of the way, but able to create the desired aesthetic.

Creating camera movement

The use of light in the video dance-making process works closely with the way that the dance is framed and how the camera moves in relation to the chorography.

In Chapter 2, we looked at how the camera interacts with the dancer's performance and discovered that movement of the camera is often the most successful way to draw viewers into the dance, engaging them in the action.

As well as the various types of camera movement such as panning, tilting and tracking, there are different approaches that you can take to actually creating that movement – for example, using so-called 'grip' equipment or going handheld. The choices you make will contribute greatly to the look and feel of your filmed video dance material.

Handheld

As the term implies, this is when you hold the camera in your hand and move with it as you film. Filming handheld has a free, spontaneous feel to it and many benefits when it comes to filming dance.

- When you handhold, you can change position quickly and react to what you are seeing in the frame, subtly and instantaneously.
- You can create complex, individualistic camera movements that might be difficult to achieve using grip equipment.
- The handheld camera often feels very like the point of view of a dancer, as the movement quality of the person operating the camera can be perceived in the shot.

Some tips for filming handheld

Aim for a fluid, yet lively sense of movement, rather than wobbly, chaotic shots. Finding the best way to move with a handheld camera takes plenty of rehearsal.

The lightweight digital cameras that are widely available are excellent for handheld filming. Smallest is not necessarily best, however, as it can be useful to have something to hold onto, and a bit of weight can make it easier to keep the camera movement steady.

If the camera is big enough, you can lean it on your shoulder rather than always hold it in your hands. This can help to keep shots steady. Some smaller cameras have attachable shoulder rests to facilitate this. Don't let the camera get stuck there, though, as this will limit your perspective on the dance.

You can also hold the camera at arm's length, down towards the ground. Remember, you don't have to look down the lens all the time as you film.

Tip!

Be aware that the height of the person filming relative to the dancer being filmed will have an effect on the frame.

Don't film handheld just because you can't be bothered to set up a tripod. If you are trying to do shots that require the camera to be completely still, or supported when panned or tilted, the results will be irritatingly shaky.

If you want a sense of movement in the shot, then go handheld; if you want absolute steadiness, then you must use a tripod or another suitable piece of grip equipment.

Grip equipment

The other most usual way to move the camera through space is to use 'grip equipment'. This term refers to a variety of different mechanical apparatus that has been specially designed and built to support and move a camera. The most common pieces of grip equipment used are as follows.

Tripod
As the name suggests, a *tripod* is a three-legged frame onto which the camera is attached, keeping it still and in position. The height of the tripod is easily adjusted and, if it has a 'fluid-head', then camera movement, such as tilting and panning, can be performed smoothly with the camera on the tripod.

Even on a no- or low-budget production, find the most professional tripod you can. This can really enhance the quality of your work. Wobbly legs and sticky head movement may be interesting on a dancer, but are more than useless on a tripod!

Dollies and tracks
A *dolly* is a tray-like platform with wheels onto which the camera can be placed. This is then usually put on the *tracks*, which are rails along which the dolly can be moved. These rails come in straight or curved sections that are joined together to make up the required shape and length of track. If the floor is even enough, an alternative is a dolly that has rubber or pneumatic wheels that can be placed directly onto the floor.

Tracking shots can be classic and gorgeous, but they must be smooth. Not all floors are suitable for placing tracks down on or using a dolly, and bumpy tracking shots are never pleasing.

Cranes and jibs
Cranes and *jibs* are larger pieces of grip equipment especially designed to lift the camera off the ground and up through space. The camera is attached directly to a 'jib' and then operated remotely, whereas a crane usually takes both camera and operator (and maybe even an focus-puller) up into the air. Cranes and jibs can give a wonderful, expansive perspective on a scene, but they tend to be expensive to hire and require specialist operators.

Sound on the shoot

As we have discussed in previous chapters of this book, the soundtrack for your video dance is an essential part of the overall work. It contributes to the creation of your on-screen world and can be made up of different elements, some of which need to be sourced on the shoot.

In Chapter 4, we followed through the process of developing a sound-track and saw who might be involved at what stage. Now, within the context of the shoot, we look at techniques for recording sound, as well as ways to use music whilst filming, if this is something that your particular production requires.

Recording sound

On video shoots, the sound and pictures are usually recorded simul-taneously onto the tape in the camera. All video cameras have built-in microphones, but these give you nothing like the control or quality that you need. You are much better advised to use an external microphone, ideally routed through a portable mixer and, if possible, work with a sound recordist.

If this sound recordist is someone who loves the challenges of their job and is excited by the possibilities of sound, then they will contribute immensely to your video dance. They will know – or find out – what sort of microphones to use and where to place them, and you can rely on them to steer you towards achieving everything that is needed audio-wise from the shoot.

Even if someone else is doing the actual recording for you, it is nevertheless important that you have an idea of some of the approaches that can be taken and the types of sounds that you may want to gather.

'If you watch a film and it is entirely out of focus, but the sound is brilliant quality, then people will say that the visuals are stylistic and the film-makers are geniuses. Try it the other way round, with the pictures crystal clear, but the sound quality poor and they will say that the film is a failure.'

John Cobban, sound designer/dubbing mixer

Actuality and synch sound

Hearing the sound of dancers' feet on the ground and the noise of their breath brings to life the images on the screen. This kind of audio is often referred to as 'actuality' sound. Actuality sound can either be recorded as 'synch sound' or as a 'wild-track'.

Synch sound is the short term for 'synchronised sound' and refers to the situation in which an image and any sound that it makes are simultaneously recorded onto the video tape. For example, if you film a shot of a pair of hands clapping, the 'synch sound' would be the noise made by the two palms coming together.

A wild-track can be made up of the same sounds as the synch, or different, but it is recorded separately from the image. You might record a wild-track of the ambient sound of the space in which you are filming, which can be very useful in the sound dub. Or, having filmed all the shots that are needed, you might record a 'wild-track' of a particular sound, just to give the sound designer some other options in the sound dub.

You should never shoot mute (that is, completely without sound). It is always best to record synch sound – and plenty of wild-tracks – on your shoot. Remember, you don't have to use these sounds in the final soundtrack, but if you have them, at least you will have the option. As we will see in Chapter 8, you can recreate all the sounds you need in a sound studio, although this can be laborious and expensive work.

If you really don't have access to any additional sound equipment, then the very least that you should do is to record using the inbuilt microphone on your camera. Whilst this will give you nowhere near the quality or control that more specialist mics and mixers – and sound recordists – will give you, at least you will have something to work with in the later stages of the soundtrack creation.

'What I need from the shoot are, if possible, the original synch sounds, as well as plenty of wild-tracks, miced as closely as possible. This gives me plenty of options to work with.'

John Cobban, sound designer/dubbing mixer

Approaches to sound recording

As we have seen, in some video dance-making processes, the chore-ography for the dancers is created to music. This may be because it is a reworking of an already existing live piece, or because it is the choreographer's preferred way of working. In other works, the entire soundtrack is devised from scratch after filming is complete and the choreographer is happy to create the movement – and the dancers perform it – without any music. Both situations require a different approach to sound recording on the shoot.

Recording with music

First, let's look at when the dancers need to perform to music on the shoot, as in many ways this can be the trickiest.

Sound-recording microphones are for the most part indiscriminate and will pick up any noises in the space. This means that, even if you just want the sounds of the dancers moving, if they are dancing to music, you will also have that on your recording.

This can cause you lots of problems. For example:

- If you want to use the synch sound in your final soundtrack, then you will be stuck with having to recreate the structure of the music in the edit, or otherwise the music will be completely messed up.
- Even if you are planning to edit the video dance material to maintain the relationship of movement to music, the quality of the music as recorded through the microphone will be poor. This is especially the case if you are playing the music through speakers.
- It is also unlikely that you will hear the sound of the dancers in motion above the level of the music. Recording both music and actuality at the same time gives you no opportunity to alter the levels of the different types of sounds, as they have been locked together.

What you really need is to have the synch sound as 'clean' as possible – that is, with little or no background noise. Then you can use the synch in whatever way you want, adding in music and other effects in the sound dub as needed.

There are some tried and tested techniques for doing this.

1.

You can hire a system which functions very like the induction loops installed for the hard of hearing in theatres. Here, the dancers wear earphones (inside their ears, so that they cannot be seen) and the music is played on a certain radio frequency that they can pick up via the earphones, but that cannot be heard by the microphones. This means that the dancers can perform to the music, whilst at the same time, the synch sound of them moving can be recorded clean.

This may seem ideal, but from what I have been told, this system is not perfect. The main reason is that the earphones do not always stay in place and the whole system is rather fiddly to set up and doesn't always work perfectly, which can be frustrating and time-consuming.

2.

A simpler technique is to place the microphone as close to the action as possible – often on the floor – and to play the music as quietly as possible, allowing the dancers to hear it, but minimising what will be picked up by the microphone.

This approach is only really successful if the same musical track to which the dancers are performing is to be the soundtrack for your video dance. In the sound dub, you can lay a 'clean' version of the music over the edited images and mix in any actuality sounds to achieve the audio balance that you want. Any music in the background of the foot and breath noises will be submerged in the clean track, but you will also have the synch sound adding life to the images.

Recording without music

In contrast to the situation described above, when there is no need for music on the shoot, then you can record synch sound on every take and use this how you wish in the edit and sound dub.

Again, any audio recorded should be as clean as possible – that is, the microphone should ideally only hear the sound of the dancers in motion and nothing else. This may still be more difficult than you would imagine.

Even if the space in which you are filming is free from outside noise, when you have a moving camera, then the sound of the track or the camera crew's feet as they move with the camera, or track, may be heard.

Often the most useful synch sound is that which is recorded very close-up to the action. This will give you the most intimate and usually most effective results. When you can, make sure that the sound recordist is able to get as close as possible into the action with his or her microphone. The microphone is usually on long pole called a boom, which is best held above the action.

It is a good idea to give yourself at least one take where the priority is to record usable sound. You might have the opportunity to do this on a medium or close-up shot when the camera is not moving.

Alternatively, do a special take for sound in which the camera is still, everything else in the space quiet and the sound recordist can go as close up to the movement as he or she needs.

It can be that the location in which you are filming is hopeless for sound. For example, there is a busy road next to it or a heating system that makes any sounds from the dancers impossible to hear.

As we saw in Chapter 5, when we looked at the practicalities of pre-production, ideally a filming location should be found that is suitable for both picture and sound recording. Of course, that is not always possible and it is usually the picture that takes priority! You may have to accept that in some situations, all that you can do is to record wild-tracks of the choreography somewhere more peaceful (time for this must be scheduled), or create all the necessary sound effects in the sound studio at a later date.

Saving time later

With all that there is to do during the shoot, it can be tempting to fall into the trap of thinking about some things, 'I'll sort that out later'. However, you will find that time is as equally precious after the shoot as you prepare for the edit. There are a few time-saving processes that can be under-taken as you film which will help the edit run smoothly. As director, if you

Tip!

It is a good idea to ask your sound designer or dubbing mixer to talk directly to the sound recordist about what he or she anticipates needing from the shoot.

are able to delegate these jobs to someone else, then they are much more likely to happen.

Labelling tapes

This is sometimes also referred to as 'marking up' the tapes. Traditionally, it is the camera assistant who will label the tapes and their boxes, as and when they have been shot.

He or she will usually also keep hold of all the shot tapes (the 'rushes') until the end of the day's filming, when the producer or director should take them into their possession and store them safely. This is something that must be agreed in advance, especially if you are moving between different locations in the course of the day. The last thing you want is confusion about who has the rushes during the shoot.

Marking up is crucial because it will help you keep track of your precious tapes. As filming progresses, it is important to record how many tapes have been shot and to give them each a unique and logical number (i.e. Tape 1, Tape 2, Tape 3). These numbers will help you know on which tape to look for a particular shot.

The label should also include the current title of the project, the name of the director and choreographer, the name of the lighting camera-person and usually also the producer and production company, if there is one.

It is a good idea to also include the date of the shoot and the location(s).

Additionally, there may be space for a brief description of which scenes or sections of material were recorded on that particular tape. This information is usually written on the box, as it's unlikely that you will fit that amount of detail onto the tape label.

On video shoots, you may find that the sound recordist assumes the responsibility of labelling the tapes, as he or she will also write information about how the sound has been recorded as a further guide for post-production.

The Truth
Choreographer: Paulo Ribeiro and Fin Walker
Director: Katrina McPherson
Lighting Camera: Jono Smith
Producers: Ricochet and Goat

Tape # 3 12/03/02

Location: Victoria Miro Gallery
Kate's solo (Paulo)
Karin's solo (Paulo)
'Grab Onto' (all dancers/Fin)

Audio: Stereo throughout.
N.B. No synch sound Karin's solo

Filming notes

Another useful practice on the shoot is to make detailed notes of everything that is filmed. Again, it is often best to ask someone else to take responsibility for this task, as you will invariably forget if you are busy directing.

Often it is the production assistant, if you have one on the shoot, who keeps these notes. He or she should confer with you to find the most useful way to record information for your purposes and to work closely with the camera assistant and sound recordist to keep track of what is on each tape.

These notes can be made with reference to the storyboard or shot-list that you are using during filming. If the production assistant keeps a record of what has been filmed, as the shoot progresses this can be compared to what was planned and that way you can ensure that you are getting what you need.

Along with describing what's been filmed, it is important for these notes to include the start and end time-code numbers of each take – or version – of each shot that is filmed.

Understanding time-code

To understand time-code, you need to know that every second of video that you watch on screen is made up of a series of individual 'frames'. In the UK, where the 'PAL' standard is used, there are twenty-five frames per second, whereas in the USA, Canada and many other parts of the world that have 'NTSC', a second of video is made up of fractionally more than twenty-nine frames per second.

Time-code is a system encoded onto the video tape which gives each of these frames a distinct number. The numbering system is based on hours, minutes, seconds, frames. A typical PAL time-code number is 03:09:25:06 – that is 3 hours, 9 minutes 25 seconds and 6 frames.

The main reason for making notes on the shoot is to help with preparing the edit, where the use of time-code becomes essential. It is the reference system by which you – and the edit system – can identify and call up specific bits of material.

As there will often be the same time-code numbers on different tapes, it is important that the filming notes (and in fact, any reference to a particular time-code number) is accompanied by the number of the tape on which it is to be found.

When filming notes are being made, as well as the list of tape and time-code numbers, it is useful to have comments on how the filming of that particular take went. These might include comments made by the choreographer, lighting cameraperson, sound recordist and the director.

Whilst as we will see, it is best to look at all the rushes afresh as preparation for the edit begins, it can be very useful to have a note of any particular comments that your collaborators have on a particular take. In the end, it can all help to guide you through the complexity of the edit.

Tip!

When you are finished in a location, leave it how you would wish to find it!

CONTENTS

CHAPTER 8

Preparation for the Edit

Editing is a multi-layered procedure that involves working with both pictures and sound through various stages. The term commonly used to describe the entire process is 'post-production', that is, everything that happens after (post) filming.

There is a great deal of work to be done between calling 'Cut!' for the final time on the last day of your shoot and sitting down to edit. And it is important work, for the preparation you do now will have an enormous impact on the success of your completed video dance.

The structure of post-production

First off, let's take an overview of the entire post-production process. The approach outlined here is based on shooting on a digital video format and designed to produce a finished video dance that could be broadcast on television or projected on a screen, shown on a monitor or even uploaded to the Internet.

The details of the type of equipment and the experience of those working with you will depend on the context in which you are making your work. As always, it is the principles and approaches explored on these pages that can hopefully provide useful guidance.

A post-production process consists of:

* looking at your filmed material (called 'viewing rushes')
* logging the material – that is, making a selection of clips and identifying these using time-code
* entering the time-code numbers into the edit system for the off-line
* 'capturing the rushes' – that is, loading the information that makes up your selected material into the edit system
* off-line editing – making decisions on the order of the material and how it should be placed together
* exporting the information that makes up your off-line edit – that is, creating an 'edit decision list' – for the on-line
* capturing your video and audio material into the on-line system
* on-line editing – adding effects and on-screen text
* producing a master from the on-line onto a high-quality format tape
* grading the tapes, altering and improving the colour
* sound dub, creating the soundtrack
* laying off the sound onto the master and safety copies.

Off-line/on-line

If you are new to the post-production process, two common terms that are often heard and can cause the confusion are 'off-line edit' and 'on-line edit'. Perhaps it is best to clarify these terms first and then to look in more detail at the other stages of the process.

It is usual to have two stages of editing – that is, the off-line and on-line. This is because both stages have a different purpose and, usually, require different equipment.

What happens in the off-line?

The off-line edit is when creative decisions are made about the overall shape of the video dance and the order in which the shots are placed.

In the off-line edit, you will be working with the material that you have selected during the viewing and logging process.

The off-line process is usually a much longer one than the on-line: time has to be allowed for lots of different options to be tried out, before a final structure is found. Ideally, the off-line uses a cheaper, simpler edit system than the on-line, and the quality of the image does not necessarily need to be as high.

For the majority of work, the most important aspect of editing is the selection of the shots and the placement of these in an order. Ultimately, in order to off-line, all you really need to be able to do is 'cut and paste' the material. Anything beyond this can be added at the on-line stage.

If an effect is fundamental to your video dance, you may need to find a way to create it already at the off-line stage, so that you can see how it affects the overall structure of the work.

To what extent you work with sound at the off-line stage is a matter of choice and dependent on the nature of your work. We will explore the different possibilities in the next chapter.

Once the off-line is complete, the data that is all the decisions that you have made in terms of your edit is transferred to the on-line edit system. The rushes (that is, the tapes that you filmed on your shoot) will then be taken into that system and the video dance you edited in the off-line will be recreated, this time at the highest possible quality.

What happens in the on-line?

The on-line is the time to concentrate on the technical aspects of your final work, to ensure that it is the best it can be.

In the on-line, you will see any effects that you have incorporated into the edit, and you might also add some effects that were not possible in the off-line, depending on what software you were using and what equipment was available.

The on-line is also where you can make colour alterations and corrections, although if there is the budget, a specific 'picture grade' is a good idea.

Any on-screen text, such as the titles and credits, are usually created and added in the on-line.

The on-line can last between a few hours and a couple of days, depending on the length of your video dance, the complexity of what you need to achieve and the size of the budget.

At the end of the on-line, the images of your video dance will be laid onto a high-quality-format tape. This is your master tape. It is from this tape that all future copies of your video dance will be made. Guard it with your life and be sure to make a safety copy at this point, even if the audio is still to be worked on in the sound dub.

Depending on the facilities available to you and the context in which you are working, you may decide that you are going to skip going into a separate on-line and produce your master tape on the same edit system as you have created your off-line edit.

This is totally acceptable, as long as you are aware of any technical limitations that a lower specification edit system might have in terms of the quality of the final master tape. If your video dance has been com-missioned by a broadcaster, then there will be specific requirements regarding the format of your master tape and you must be sure of these before you decide on how you are going to work.

Failure to abide by these specific requirements can result in a massive overspend on your budget, as you may well end up needing to reformat your final video dance. Be sure that you know well in advance what you are expected to be delivering. Check the technical requirements with the editor and make sure that you understand them and that what you have planned for is correct.

Even if you do not have access to an on-line, it is essential to set aside time at the end of your editing period to focus on maximising the technical quality of your finished video dance. At some point, you have to stop making editorial adjustments to your work and move on to the completion stage. Scheduling an on-line forces you to bring the off-line to a close.

How long to edit?

As we saw in Chapter 5, it is important to make a production plan for your project, and this usually involves working back from the date by which you want or need to have your video dance complete. As part of this, you need to estimate how long you will want to spent off-lining, as well as how long you need to complete the on-line and sound dub. As always, it is very much dependent on the nature of the work and who you are working with.

As regards off-line editing, people work in different ways. Some teams like to spend weeks on the off-line edit, trying out lots of different options and taking time to look and reflect. Others like to work more quickly, or must do so for budget and schedule reasons. Even so, the edit usually takes several times as long as the shoot.

Personally, I like to work quickly in the off-line, as I feel that it helps the editor and I to stay energised and the work to stay fresh. This means that, whilst the entire post-production process, including sound dub, on-line and grade, may take months, the actual off-line edit, where the major creative and structural decisions are made, is relatively short.

To make the schedule possible, I ensure that I have a detailed log and a clear plan of what I am trying to achieve before even setting foot in the off-line edit suite.

'In the editing room, I am pulling out from the material aspects of the ideas that took me through the shooting. You have to stay the course with a work, you know. The longer it takes to make, the harder it is to stay the course.'

Elliot Caplan, director

Preparing to edit

At the end of filming, you will gather up the rushes tapes, hopefully clearly labelled and with well-kept notes attached, detailing their contents. Now is the time to take them home and watch them through.

It is essential to make copies of these tapes. The camera tapes from your shoot are extremely precious, containing unrepeatable moments of performance – and the last thing you want to do is damage them whilst you are spooling back and forth through them as you view the material.

Moreover, if you have filmed on a high-end professional video format, it would be expensive to sit in front of a video player that can play these and view your material over several days. So, the safest, cheapest and by far best option is to transfer all your rushes for viewing onto a more available format.

What format you use depends on whether you are going to log the material using a computer software or by hand. In the former case, you will need the copies of your tapes to be 'clones' of the originals – that is, to have identical time-code and numbers to those on your original camera tapes. (See Chapter 7 for an explanation of time-code.)

Alternatively, you may need the time-code made visible on the picture. This is called 'burnt-in time code' (BITC) or a 'window dub', so that you can log by viewing on a monitor and writing down numbers by hand. These numbers will then be entered into the system on which you are going to do the off-line edit of your video dance.

Viewing rushes

You may have already watched the rushes during the shoot, either in camera in the course of the filming day, or at the end of each day. Although potentially a risky business, looking at what has just been filmed during the shoot is sometimes unavoidable, and its usefulness out-weighs the risk of damaging your material or holding up the filming process.

However, even if you have already seen some or all of what you have filmed during the shoot, examining the material at the beginning of post-production is a very different experience.

Using the carefully kept tape logs from the shoot, it would be possibly to cut corners by going straight to the shots that have been marked up as the best and only looking at the other filmed material if something appears to be missing, or is not as good as is indicated in the notes.

When I start to prepare for the edit, however, I like to look at all the filmed material at least once through in its entirety. This allows me a valuable overview of everything that was filmed and gives me an impression of the strengths and weaknesses of the material, away from the intensity of the shoot.

Viewing rushes is best done on a television or monitor, at home or in your office, not in an expensive edit suite. That way you can take as much time as you need, and it is time well spent, as viewing and then selecting the material for the edit is the most important part of the overall process.

Selecting and logging

Having viewed all the material in its entirety at least once, making notes as you watch, it is now time to get down to the serious business of selecting – or 'logging' – the material.

At its most rudimentary, editing is about choosing the best shots and putting them in an order. It is now that this process really begins, as you are now deciding which images will be there in front of you and the editor when you start to piece your video dance together.

Whatever editing software you are using, you need to break the filmed material down into 'clips'. These may vary in length from a few seconds (check how short your edit system can deal with in terms of digitising) to longer sequences (but remember that there is little merit in sifting through long tracts of material in the edit).

Now, as you watch through the rushes, you will need to stop and start more and look and listen in greater detail. You will use the time-code numbers of each frame or second to identify the start and finish (the 'in' and 'out') points of each clip. It is the material in between these two points that become a clip and that will be taken into the edit system.

There are two ways in which you can log your rushes.

1. Use a logging software on a computer hooked up to a tape player. This needs your transfers to have identical time-code to the camera tape that it is a copy of. As you play the tape, you can mark an in and an out point in the places of your choice using the software controls. At the end of the process, the software will produce a list of all the numbers that represent your choices of the material that you want to be taken into the off-line edit.

2. The other way is to log by hand, watching the material and reading the burnt-in time-code numbers on the screen, as described earlier. The process is the same: you mark the in and out points of the clips that you are selecting, but you must write these numbers down and then they in turn must be entered into the off-line edit system.

How you work is dependent on what facilities you have access to. The purpose and skill of logging remain the same.

We saw in Chapter 7 how, on the shoot, each tape must be labelled clearly and given a unique number. When you are logging, you must use these tape numbers to identify which tape you are selecting material from.

Over many different rushes tapes, there will be several identical time-code numbers. This means that you need to make it clear which tape you are referring to when you are making your choices. In most logging software, you will be asked to enter the correct tape number when you load a different tape into the system.

At all stages of logging, take care with time-code and tape numbers. Mistakes with digits can waste lots of precious edit time.

Shots become clips

A word now about the difference between a 'shot' and a 'clip'. In the context of editing, I like to use the term 'clip' rather than shot. This is because it helps to make the distinction between the shots that were planned and filmed on the shoot, and the material that is actually taken into the edit.

Whilst some of these 'clips' may be complete 'shots', many others will be sections or 'clips' taken from shots. For the sake of clarity, I will use the term 'clip' from this point on in the book. However, some of the other practitioners who are quoted do use the term 'shot' when talking about the editing process.

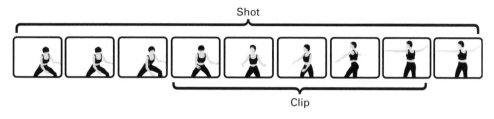

Figure 8.1 **A shot becomes a clip**

Unless the whole point of a particular shot is to have it as an uninterrupted take, for example, a long tracking shot, you do not necessarily need to take entire shots into the edit.

It might be that only a few seconds of a particular take works really well, in which case, just select those moments, marking an in and an out point at either end of the section. As I say, this might not be an entire shot, but you will find that these fragments are very useful for editing.

As we will see, it is the transition between different clips that creates energy and dynamic. Even in the case of the continuous shot idea, you may find in any case that you end up breaking it up with other material to alter the pace of the edit. So, if one part of a continuous shot is brilliant, select it and use it, even if another part of the take has not worked out.

'In a shot, I'm looking for an interesting relationship between the camera, the dancers' movement, and the space. I'm looking for dynamic in and out points. And I'm looking for ways in which that one shot will lead to another shot in an exciting way.'

Simon Fildes, editor

Active logging

Whilst logging your material, you need to keep in mind what the intention of the work is. This will help to inform your choices of what to select and what you reject. Throughout the process of making video dance, there is a fine balance to be struck between pursuing the line of enquiry that you set out to explore and allowing the work to guide you in a new direction. It seems to me that nowhere is this more the case than in the edit.

You will often find that the material you have in front of you at the end of the filming process is very different from what you imagined. In many ways, this is the true excitement of making video dance. You can – and need to – plan everything in great detail, but what actually happens in the 'performance' of filming will have qualities and characteristics unique to that particular moment in time.

One of the skills of viewing and logging rushes is to remain open to this uniqueness. Look with energy and imagination, as if seeing the material for the very first time. Ask yourself these questions:

*   What catches your eye?
*   What does it make you feel?
*   What sort of variety is there in the material?
*   Does the material suggest a way of structuring it?
*   Are there some interesting sounds?

Don't just select the takes in which everything went as planned. These will not always be the moments where the dance and filming really came together to create something extraordinary that might add an unexpected edge to your edited video dance.

Remember also that you are not necessarily looking for entire takes of shots that were 'successful'; you will find that in the edit you can – and will often – use fragments of shots.

Logging your rushes is an intensive experience and, in order to stay fresh and concentrated, I tend to work in short bouts. It can be also be a frustrating, uncomfortable and sometimes even boring task, as you must look at every moment that was filmed and relive the highs and lows of your shoot.

But persevere and do the job thoroughly. Knowing your rushes intimately and making good, clear choices about what you take into the edit suite will have an enormous impact on the edit and the outcome of the work.

Limit your palette

It is important to limit what you select for the edit. On a purely practical level, there is often a finite amount of material that you can take into the edit, as determined by the capacity of the particular digital editing system that you are using.

Even if the system allows you to work with a great deal of material, I urge you to set your own limits. It is a good idea to discuss this with the editor.

The last thing you want to be doing in the edit suite is trawling though big chunks of material or many different versions of the same shot. Even in the cheapest off-line, the meter will be running and edit systems (and editors, if you are working with one) are expensive things to hire.

Don't forget that you can always go back to the rushes to fetch something that you left out at this point. This is especially the case if you have well-written log sheets and, through viewing your rushes in detail, are familiar with all your filmed material.

Naming your clips

As we saw in Chapter 3, it is very useful to name the different sections of material that you are filming. This helps everyone know what section is being referred to during rehearsals, pre-production and filming.

When it comes to preparing for the edit, however, it is best to discard these names and make up new ones for the clips and edited sections. The reason for this is that it is really important to be thinking about the edit in terms of the material that you have in front of you, rather than what was choreographed and filmed. By renaming your material in the edit, you can help this process of moving away from the live event.

Capturing

Once the logging process is complete and you have a list of all the clips that you want to use in the edit, it is time to take your selected rushes into the computer on which you are going to off-line.

This process is usually called 'capturing' and involves each tape being played into the computer, with the sections of material you have chosen being transferred into the off-line system.

You can see now why it is so important that your tapes are clearly labelled, as the software will request each tape individually, according to the data that it has been given.

If you are working with an editor, he or she may want to oversee the capturing process, as it gives him or her the chance to watch and listen to the material before editing begins. In my experience, editors often like the chance to do this alone, without the over-anxious director breathing down their neck.

Who is in the edit suite?

'I found out that I am collaborative by nature in that I was quite happy to have the choreographer in the edit and if they had a good idea, we would try it. At that point, you felt you had the final say as a director but, when you had built up a working relationship with certain choreographers, what they had to say was always interesting.'

Ross MacGibbon, director

The off-line edit is when the work really comes together and the true nature of the video dance emerges.

It is also the time when decisions become final. Ultimately you are working towards one version of the work and by the end of the off-line, there is really no going back. Therefore, deciding who is involved and how they input in this part of the process is crucial.

The most usual ways to collaborate in the edit are as follows.

- The director and editor work closely together, with the choreographer coming into the edit at regular intervals to give feedback. The choreographer will probably have seen all the rushes and will have helped in their selection.
- Both choreographer and director collaborate full-time in the edit, working with an editor whose contribution is mainly operating the edit system.
- A director and choreographer work together in the edit, with the director also operating the edit system.

As always, there are pros and cons of all three situations, and your choice of how to work will be dependent on your particular project and the skills and interests of those involved.

In many respects, the choice of how to work depends on what sort of input you want the editor to have. A skilled and enthusiastic editor can contribute enormously to your video dance. As with any creative collaborator, you need to be sure that you share the same vision.

However, I have a theory that, when it comes to editing, two's company and three's a crowd, which means, if both choreographer and director want to be in the edit suite, if you collaborate with an editor, then you may find yourselves involved in many long and frustrating three-way conversations, as you try to reach an agreement on where to place a shot.

'Where we [Rosemary Lee and Peter Anderson, director] get collaborative again is in the edit. I think it's very hard, especially when we're working with an editor on the machine. It means we work quite slowly taking our time to come to a consensus. We may have a Rosie version and a Pete version of little edited phrases that we go between until we finally agree. But everyone works differently and this is just our way that was right for us at the time.'

Rosemary Lee, choreographer/director

An alternative is to work with an editor who is happy just to operate the system and to withhold all opinions, although I would suggest that, in this day and age when there are plenty of straightforward off-line edit systems available, if this is your preferred way of working, one of you should learn to use the software and save an editor a rather tedious job!

In my experience, editing is best when there are two people working closely, with any others coming in at predetermined intervals to view the work in progress and to give feedback. In the video dance works that I direct, I always collaborate with editor Simon Fildes, whose input into the process is crucial. The choreographers I have worked with have always appreciated this and have been happy to take a more peripheral, yet equally essential role.

As part of this process, however, it is very important that we all share a vision of what we are trying to achieve with our video dance and that the choreographers have also had the chance to view all the rushes, so that they too are aware of all the different options for the edit. (Simon prefers only to see what I select to take into the off-line.)

Finally, if your role has been as both choreographer and director of your video dance, you may feel that you also want to edit the work entirely yourself.

If you do choose this solitary route, be aware that working alone can be hard and that the creative side of editing benefits from having more than one brain involved. This is especially the case if you have choreographed, directed and maybe even shot your video dance, as you will unavoidably be very close to the material and may benefit enormously from scrutiny by the fresh eyes of an editor.

Time spent in the edit

Whoever is involved in the edit – choreographer, director, editor – it is a good idea to discuss at the beginning if you are both, or all, going to be in the edit all the time, or if you are going to come and go a bit.

When working with Simon, I find it is very beneficial to leave the edit for periods of time, letting him get on with what we have discussed. After an agreed amount of time, or when a certain task has been carried out,

I will come back in and together we will look at the results and decide where to go from there.

This approach has a number of benefits.

- It gives the editor some time and space to work without the director breathing down his or her neck.
- It creates space, enabling the director to see the material with fresh eyes on his or her return to the suite.
- It allows the director some precious time out of the edit suite and a chance to sort out ongoing production issues such as compiling the credits, writing marketing text and organising the premiere.

CONTENTS

CHAPTER 9

Choreography of the Edit

I relish the moment of sitting down in front of the edit system, just me and the editor, ready to start shaping a new video dance. After the very public and heavily populated pre-production and filming, this feels like a much more intimate and directly creative part of the process.

There is also the sense that, in amongst the clips in front of us, our video dance is there, its final form and character waiting to be released. It is an exciting moment.

The first cut

For many artists, the best part of making video dance is the editing. It is through the juxtaposition of different shots and sounds that the work assumes its emotional impact, as characters are revealed by fragments of action and as the viewer is drawn through a series of events and states.

The significance of a moment, or movement and the interaction between different performers can be explored, as time is slowed down, stretched, speeded up, repeated or stopped through the editing.

At its simplest, editing is about placing one shot after another. Whilst technology has evolved to the point that, rather than sticking pieces of celluloid together, what we are doing as we edit is shifting digital representations of data up and down a computer time-line, the art, craft and grammar of editing has remained consistent through the history of film and video.

These constants apply whatever the nature of your work and the approaches you have taken to filming and editing. However, they are not rules to be adhered to, but rather guidelines to follow: the magic is in the original way that your video dance choreography takes shape in the edit.

'Editing is where the work comes together. I can only take ideas so far with the camera. It's satisfying up to a certain point, but it's studying an image and looking for possibilities of where to take that image, and what comes first and what comes second – it's the relation of one image following another – that's what really excites me.'

Elliot Caplan, director

Once capturing is complete, have a look and listen to what has been taken into the edit system. This is a chance for you to assess the palette of clips at your disposal, separated out from that which was discarded. Do this with the others – the editor and choreographer – who will be involved in the edit.

Watching the material together now gives an opportunity to clarify your approach, updated with any new thoughts that you have had as a result of what you have seen and heard whilst viewing and logging. It is also the time to make an initial plan of how you are going to work.

There are different ways to start editing. For example, you can begin by roughly sketching out the entire video dance, laying down shots on the time-line (see explanation of time-line next), but without going into too much detail of how exactly these will be edited together. This will give you a sense of the overall shape of the work, and you can then go and work on the different sections in detail.

Alternatively, begin by editing some short sections in quite fine detail, saving them separately as individual sequences. Once a few of these have been completed, lay them down one after the other on the time-line to get an idea of the overall shape of the work.

Whatever approach you take – and you can vary this in different sections – your method of editing should be determined by the ideas you are working with. It is also important that you do not simply follow through the plan that you made before you filmed, but rather that you look at and respond to the material anew.

'When I get in the editing room after working with a series of ideas on camera, I now have the chance to try to fit them together in different ways, and I experiment a lot. I don't go and say: "Okay, now this is shot 1 and now I just attach shot 2 and I look for a pleasant place to do that and then I go to shot 3 . . ." It's never like that.'

Elliot Caplan, director

What is a time-line?

In computer-based edit systems, the time-line represents the structure and duration of your video dance.

When you are editing, you are working with graphical representations, appearing as horizontal strips, that symbolise the in and out points of the time-code of your video dance material, enabling the computer to play the clips that you have selected.

As you edit, you place these graphical representations onto the time-line, where they can be altered and reordered indefinitely. A time-line will usually have a number of these horizontal strips, representing the different layers of picture and sound that make up your edit.

By the end of the edit, your final version of the time-line will hold all the information that is needed to recreate your video dance when it is laid off onto video tape.

Figure 9.1 **A time-line on a digital editing system**

Finding the structure

As we have seen many times throughout this book, it is very important to have a clear idea for your work. This helps you to develop the choreography, to choose locations and to decide how to frame and shoot your material.

The idea for your work also guides you in the edit. Even if by the end of the off-line edit, the completed work ends up being very different from how you had imagined, knowing your intention will help you to find a structure and start to work in the editing suite.

We saw in Chapter 1 that there are many different types of idea upon which a video dance can be based, and each will suggest a different way of finding a structure in the edit.

- If your video dance is based on a narrative, then you can start by laying down the building blocks of the story: the key scenes or events.
- If the purpose of your video dance is to recreate the structure of the choreography as it was performed live, the shape of the edit will be determined by this, at least initially.
- If your video dance is based on a piece of music, then the soundtrack should go onto the time-line first, providing a structure onto which the pictures can be laid.

- Another way to think about the structure of the edit is to let the material itself guide you. Explore the effect of simply placing shots side by side on the time-line. You will find that some juxtapositions work really well and immediately suggest the next move to make.

'I probably spend the first few days of any edit just looking at the material, hardly making any edits at all. What I'll be doing is making little marks, in and out points on each clip to remind myself, and I'll make a mental note: "mmm . . . that was an interesting clip." Then, if I'm feeling confident about a particular section, I may start putting the material on the time-line and having a look and seeing how the pieces come together.'

Simon Fildes, editor

Working with clips

As we have seen, editing is fundamentally about laying down one clip after another on the time-line. How you choose to do this is determined by the overall idea for the work and the structure that you are setting out to create.

Knowing at what point to start a clip and at what point to end it is key to this creative process. The length, shape and character of each clip that you use will vary immensely.

When you are deciding where to start and finish a clip, you will be looking for distinctive moments. What these moments are is infinitely variable.

The start (or in point) of a clip may be:

- the beginning of a movement that catches your eye, even before the subject of the frame becomes recognisable
- the point at which a body part enters the frame
- the moment at which whatever is in the frame comes into focus, or not!

A clip may also follow a movement through space, or it might consist of a movement passing through a static frame.

The end (or out point) of a clip may come:

- when the frame becomes empty, or when the frame is completely filled by action
- at the moment that two figures make, or lose, contact
- the instance a foot stamps the floor or a body part spins round into or out of focus.

Transitions

As well as finding the best order for them, you also need to decide how you want to transition between each of these clips – that is, to go from one to the next.

The two most commonly used transitions in video dance editing are the 'cut' and the 'dissolve'. They have very different effects.

Cuts

A cut is the immediate and complete transition from one clip to the next. The cut is the most important tool of editing.

A large part of the skill and art of editing is to find the optimum point at which to cut between two images, in order to create the impact that you want. The effect of a cut can be significantly changed by altering the edit point by a few frames or fractions of a second.

Dissolves

A 'dissolve' is when one clip is gradually replaced by another. This transition can take place over a couple of frames, or over seconds or even minutes!

A dissolve lasting only a few frames is sometime referred to a 'soft cut', as the eye will be unable to see the transformation of one image to the next, but there will be a sense that the transition is not as immediate as a cut.

According to the conventions of film grammar, a dissolve implies a shift to a different time and/or place.

You can create interesting effects with superimpositions, in which one or more video images are layered (or part dissolved) over each other.

Some people love dissolves and soft cuts, but I do not share their enthusiasm, except when they fulfil a very clearly designed and considered function. Dissolves can look rather obvious and are often resorted to when the best place to cut has not been found.

Those in favour of dissolves argue that dissolves help to create a sense of flow between different shots. However, this fluidity can be equally – and often better – achieved by selecting the right clips and finding the best moment on which to cut between them. Very often dissolves are used to cover up bad or lazy editing.

Working with sound in the edit

Early on in the off-lining process, you must decide how you are going to work with sound. Let us look at some of the options.

- Some video dance-makers choose not to work with any sound at all in the off-line, preferring to concentrate on finding the rhythms and structure of the visuals and leaving all sound work until after the picture edit is complete.
- For others, music is fundamental to the creative editing process, whether the tracks used are a guide to be re-recorded at a later stage or the actual music that will become the final soundtrack.
- Actuality sounds, recorded whilst filming, can also be incorporated into the off-line, forming a useful basis for the soundtrack, which is then created in the sound dub.

'One of the things that I wanted to do with *Birds* was to prove to myself that you can choreograph purely through film editing and achieve something which has all the qualities that a dance person might require from dance, like rhythm and structure and a fascination with action. So, in the edit, I began with the idea that you have got to start with the rhythms of the action itself and not get distracted by rhythms that are going on within the music. I thought we had to make something that worked purely as visual music first of all, just the images and no sound.'

David Hinton, director

Tip!

Be careful if you use music as a guide in your off-line, especially if it is a track that you don't yet have the rights to use. It is very easy to become attached to the way that a particular sequence of images works with a piece of music, and it can be very hard to let this go when you replace it with the actual music that you are to use.

Music

You may choose to work with music in the off-line edit because your intention is to maintain the continuity of the choreography as it happened live. Because the dance was created to music, then the music also becomes the soundtrack to the video dance, with the relationship between sound and movement being maintained.

In this approach, the music track is the first thing to put on the time-line, with the video dance clips that contain the appropriate sections of choreography then placed down in synch with the music.

In re-works, the music is often re-scored for the video dance version for, as we explored in Chapter 1, the structure of the screen version will have a very different structure to the live choreography. This usually happens after the picture edit has been finished, although some of the original tracks might be used as a guide in the edit.

Music can also provide the starting point for the edit with works created originally and only for the screen. For example:

- A musical track, either especially composed for the video dance or pre-existing, can be laid onto the time-line with the video dance then built up by laying shots onto the time-line, guided by the structure provided by the musical track.
- If it is already recorded, then this music may be fixed. However, if you are collaborating with a composer, then there can be some toing and froing, with the musical tracks being adapted to respond to how the visuals are working when the two are placed together.

Actuality

Even if you do not want to work with music in the edit, either because it is not going to be part of the final soundtrack or because it is going to be recorded or sourced at a later stage, its usually advisable to incorporate actuality sounds into the off-line edit.

As we have already seen, actuality can be either synch sounds attached to a visual image of an action, or audio recorded separately as a 'wild-track.' Either way, in dance, the actuality sounds are usually the sound of feet on the floor and breathing, but they may also include other noises from the location.

There is an enormous difference between working with and without the actuality sounds in the off-line. Try it out and you will see that the images and edits have a much greater impact and sense of energy when there is audio attached.

'It can be really helpful if the editor has laid down some sounds and wild-tracks in the edit. It gives me something to work with, otherwise I am starting from a complete blank. This is more so the case in dance film, where there is no dialogue to work off.'

John Cobban, sound designer/dubbing mixer

One approach to using actuality sounds in the off-line edit is to retain any synch attached to the clips and, as you build up your visual clips on the time-line, the sound will take on a shape of its own. This aural pattern can then form the basis of your soundtrack.

A good piece of advice is, if you have a close and a wide version of a particular section of synch sound, lay both onto the audio layers of the time-line. This will give the sound designer or dubbing mixer the choice of which to use, and he or she may end up incorporating a mix of the two into your soundtrack.

You should also lay in wild-tracks of sound from your rushes that you feel are appropriate for different sections of the edited work. These wild-tracks can be very useful in the sound dub, as they suggest atmospheres and energies that you may imagine being enhanced by the soundtrack.

Remember, what you do sonically in the off-line will serve as a valuable guide, both to you and the off-line editor, and to the sound designer and/or dubbing mixer. However, whatever you do can, and most probably will, be completely altered in the sound dub.

The sound–image relationship

Whether you are working with music or actuality sound, or both, or none, there is much to explore in terms of the relationship between the picture and sound as you edit.

As we have seen, the off-line is all about choosing which order to lay down a series of visual images and then finding the right moment and way to transition between them. How the audio is then placed in relationship to the visual also has great impact.

For example, the audio can:

- change at exactly the same time as the picture
- change before or after the picture transition
- remain constant throughout the picture transitions
- change whilst the picture remains the same.

Although the video camera records picture and sound together on tape, once you get into the edit suite, these two elements can very easily be separated. The time-line has layers for sound and for picture, and this means that the structure of the visuals and of the audio of your video dance can differ greatly.

Whilst the greater part of your soundtrack design will happen outside the off-line edit, either by the composer writing and recording music or by the sound designer in the dub, for many editors it is crucial to begin drawing on the creative possibilities of how sound and image work together at the off-line stage.

Editing concerns

Editing often feels like the most creative part of making video dance. What happens when you place one clip after another, then add another, is at the heart of editing and there are endless possibilities to try out and many issues to consider, in terms of how you put your material together.

Here are some things to think about as you edit (in no particular order).

- What is the overall effect that you are trying to create, and is each choice that you make contributing towards this?
- Are you looking to create a sense of speed and energy that pulls the viewer through the movement? Or do you want the viewer to study each shot carefully and in detail? (You can do both at different points in the edit.)
- How is the relationship between the performers revealed and developed through the editing?
- How can you create changes of pace in the edit?
- In which order do you want the viewer to receive the material, and how does this effect their perception of the material?
- How are the dancers introduced? Are they gradually revealed, or perhaps they are gradually concealed?
- How is space featured? Is it gradually revealed or concealed? Does it start empty, becoming filled?
- How are different spaces and locations related?
- Does the structure of the video dance present a journey inward, or a journey outward?
- What is the effect if a shot is repeated, twice, three times, many times? Or if we see the same moment from a different angle?
- How do the sound and the images relate to each other?
- What role is colour playing in the way that you are ordering your material?
- Think about the size of the different shots: are you cutting between shots of similar sizes, or making extreme changes in scale?

Creating flow

'At the end of a shot, I'd be looking for a point which may be an unresolved action, i.e. a foot hitting the floor, and I will cut just before the foot hits the floor. That could lead into another action in the incoming shot that might echo this, or start to build up a rhythm.'

Simon Fildes, editor

Whatever the idea for the work, and no matter what the style of choreography, one of my own priorities in the editing of video dance is to achieve a sense of flow. As we work together, editor Simon Fildes and

I are always looking for ways to link the images that draw the viewer through the action. This is whether we are editing to maintain the continuity of the live dance, or creating montage by juxtaposing images from completely different points in time and space.

The choice of clips and the order in which they come in a sequence of video dance material, has a great effect on the flow of a sequence.

Any clip, unless both the content and the frame are completely static, will contain a sense of motion. This may result from the dancer's body, or body part, passing through the frame, or it may be the result of a specific camera movement, or the combination of both dancer and camera movement.

When you are placing one clip after the other to edit a sequence, you need to look at the direction of the motion of each individual clip and allow this to follow through into the next shot. Over several shots, this will create a sense of flow. It is as if a line of momentum is being passed from one shot to the next, although what actually carries that movement, for example, the dancer or camera movement – will vary.

As well as choice of clip and the order that they come in, finding the right point at which to make a transition between shots is also very important when creating flow in your editing.

What you need to do is to 'cut on the movement'. This means that the out point of the outgoing shot, the moment at which you leave it, comes before the movement in that shot is completed, and the in point of the incoming shot, the moment at which you enter, happens after the movement in that shot has begun.

Editing in this way draws on the fact that the viewer will finish off the movement in their mind's eye. As this perception combines with the tension created by not always allowing each shot to complete, it gives rise to a very active and compelling viewing experience.

A common fault when editing dance is that the movement contained within a shot, or the movement of the camera, or both, is allowed to start and to finish before each transition (cut or dissolve) is made. This will prevent any sense of flow building up in a sequence.

This is not to say that there should be no pauses in the flow of a sequence. Moments of stillness – and silence – that break the flow create interest and intrigue and can make the viewer more aware of the movement that has and will happen.

Creating pace

Another very important element of editing is pace. Again, this is affected by the nature of the individual clips, as well as by how they are placed in sequence.

Pace is concerned with the speed of the edit. Every video dance sets its own pace.

- Some are contemplative, with a slow pace that allows each image to develop and be studied, before moving onto the next.
- Other works have a rapid, speedy pace, cutting between short clips every few seconds or combining high-energy, fast-moving clips.

A well-structured video dance work usually employs a variety of paces through its different sections.

The perception of pace as a viewer is very subjective, as what has come before or after a certain section will affect your experience of it. For example, a static wide shot coming straight after a sequence of short, glimpsed images will seem much slower than the same shot placed directly after another slow-moving shot.

When you are looking back at what you have edited, often the strongest impression you will have will be that it feels 'too slow' or, less usually, 'too fast'. This is all about the pace.

There are various things to consider when working on the pace of your edit.

If a sequence feels too slow, look at the length of the individual shots.

It might be that by trimming them back, either at the in or at the out point, or both, you will find that you can speed up the edit considerably.

If trimming does not bring the results you are looking for, then try losing some shots.

It always surprises me how often dropping a clip completely works to pick up the speed of a sequence and how quickly you will stop missing it when the sequence starts to work.

'One has all kinds of choices in terms of how long to leave an image on the screen. A thirtieth of a second? Several seconds? A minute? When you leave something on the screen, what you're doing is you're giving the viewer an opportunity to look at it. If I leave something on the screen, I'm doing so because I know there are things there that I want you to see.'

Elliot Caplan, director

Creating story

Even if your video dance is not based a specific story, you will inevitably, at some level, be working with narrative. This is because video dance, as it is commonly defined, has the movement of human beings as its subject, and where we see people, we usually try to make sense of their behaviour by creating stories.

As we have seen in earlier chapters, it might be that the starting point of your video dance was formal, musical, visual or conceptual.

Nevertheless, when you start to edit images featuring bodies in motion and people interacting, you will be faced with the challenge that the material will present stories and relationships.

Don't despair, however, for this is a wonderful thing. This interplay, some-times even tension, between the formal concerns of video-making and the unavoidably human nature of dance is what makes this hybrid art form such an exciting and compelling one.

But if telling stories is not really your intention, do you really need to pay attention to this aspect of the work as you edit?

At one level, I would say, yes. Your choice of material, the order the clips come in and the transitions between them will have an impact in terms of creating a narrative, whether intentionally or not.

For example, if you use a close-up shot of a dancer's face, the direction in which he or she is looking in relation to an incoming shot of another dancer's face, or body part, will inevitable create meaning in the viewer's mind. Your choice of whether to cut before or after a hand comes to rest on a shoulder might be based on a rhythmical concern, but it will also alter how the work is read and understood.

Whilst your edit decisions may be determined by ideas or concepts other than by story, you still need to be aware that the human content is really the most powerful element of your video dance work, and that is often what will communicate before anything else.

'When I was directing the screen version of Rosemary Butcher's *Touch the Earth*, after the opening solo, two figures, a male and a female, walk into the space towards the person that was the focus of the action. In an early edit, after seeing the two figures enter, I cut to a mid-shot of the male dancer and then continued on. When Rosemary saw this, she was very shocked as she saw this as the female character's dance, and my cutting to the male dancer first had made it the male's dance. This shows the importance of the order the material to the understanding of a sequence.'

Bob Lockyer, producer/director

Repetition

When we are thinking about ways of editing video dance material, it is important to realise that there is always the opportunity to really push the boundaries of people's expectations of video dance.

In Chapter 2, we explored the difference between filming and editing to maintain the structure of the live choreography and the 'montage' approach, in which shots from different contexts are juxtaposed to create a whole new choreography, one that is unique to the screen.

As we saw, montage frees you from the constraints of what happened 'live'. This can be taken onto new levels, by also exploring what happens to the perception of time and movement when this montage includes repeated and altered patterns of material.

When working with digital, non-linear editing systems, you can very easily copy clips of video dance material. This 'cut and paste' process makes it possible to experiment with new ways of structuring dance that take editing beyond finding the best way of transitioning between two different shots to create compelling energy on the screen.

In many ways, this approach to editing is very like creating music; the clips become like notes, phrases or samples that can be repeated and looped, altering slightly over time, or transforming from one texture to another by replacing shots, frame by frame.

Macro- and micro-editing

As you work in the off-line, you will return many times to the different scenes or sections of your video dance. As the shape of your video dance evolves, you will also find that your attention will shift between the micro and the macro, that is, at some points your focus will be on the effect of altering the images and sound, frame by frame – at a 'micro' level – whereas at other times you will be looking at the overall effect of a scene or section, or the shape or 'arc' of the entire video dance work – working at a 'macro' level.

At this stage, it is useful to remember that video dance material is made up of a series of still frames that represent the images captured by the camera. As we saw in Chapter 7, when discussing time-code, there are either twenty-five frames or twenty-nine frames per second (depending on whether you are working in the PAL or NTSC standard). It is the 'playing back' of these images that recreates the movement captured by the camera.

In general, when your video dance is viewed, the focus is on the overall effect of the motion created by these frames rushing past. However, there will be times in the off-line when you find that the biggest impact you can have on your work is by losing or adding a frame, or rather, altering the edit by one twenty-fifth of a second!

'I usually do the first assembly on my own, with the editor. Then the choreographer will come in and we will look at it together and say things like: "Well, for me, this bit is mostly about pace and rhythm", or "What emotion needs to come out here?" or "This bit needs to be more exciting and if I cut that faster, it will probably make it more exciting, so let's have a look at that." You are looking at the arc of the film and what is coming across and then you are fine-cutting and I do all that in consultation with the choreographer.'

Ross MacGibbon, director

Special effects

Beyond the selection, ordering and cutting of images that is at the heart of editing, there are other ways of treating your material that will affect its impact on the viewer.

Although cameras often offer lots of special effects – for example, black and white, pixilation, juddery shutter-speed – it is wiser to film all your material without effects. Even if you are very sure that you want everything to be in black and white, or slow motion, or to have some other distinctive look, it is better, if possible, to leave any alterations of the material to post-production. That way you can see how things look when the work is edited together and, if you change your mind about plans for a certain effect, you can always go back to your rushes.

The secret of the skilful use of effects is that they should not feel like an effect to the viewer. That is to say, they must be integral to the work and essential to what it communicates. For that reason, any effect should really be part of your initial idea and included in the development of the work.

Every editing system will also offer an array of different effects. As these are constantly being upgraded and added to by the software manufacturers, there is little point in detailing them all here. If you are interested, check out the tutorial supplied on your edit system. It will demonstrate all the available effects on your system.

A word of warning first, and this goes for both in-camera and post-production effects: discovering a 'new' effect is very exciting and can blind you to the fact that countless other artists will have already used – and even over-used – that same one. You may end up creating a look for your video dance that has been seen in a large proportion of the work already out there.

Slow motion

The one effect that is used so regularly that it is often not even considered to be an effect is slow motion. Slow motion – or 'slo-mo' – is very popular with video dance makers.

Watching human movement running even a little slower than normal is usually very beautiful and can have emotional power. You see the shape of the movement more clearly, the dancer and camera movement feels smooth and suspended, as the slow motion creates an almost gravity-free effect.

However, slow motion is also an over-used effect and can feel like a cover-up of poorly crafted choreography and weak camera work.

It can also seem rather odd to have only one slo-mo shot in amongst a sequence of footage at 'normal' speed.

Rather than quickly resorting to using slow-motion effect, see if you can achieve the same fluidity and clarity through the quality of the images you create on the shoot and the style with which you edit.

'You can change the speed and dynamic of a sequence by altering the length of the shots and the type of shots you use. If you want to slow things down, you can usually do so by editing, rather than having to resort to slo-mo. Likewise, if you want to speed things up, unless your intention is to create comedy, I wouldn't use fast-motion effects. I would try to do it through the editing.'

Simon Fildes, editor

Keeping time in the edit

Time management is as important in the edit as it is on the shoot. It is easy to get caught up in the detail of a single section and to forget about the other areas that need to be worked on.

There is no point in endlessly perfecting your opening section, then finding that you have run out of editing time to complete your video dance.

For that reason, it is good to make a plan for the time you have in the off-line. Before you start off, calculate how many days you have, what you need to achieve, and from this you can estimate how much time you can afford to spend on each section, as well as considering the whole.

'I think you have to go with gut feelings a lot of the time. And don't get too attached to things. If something is not working, then lose it. "If in doubt, chuck it out." I think that's a good philosophy.'

Simon Fildes, editor

Feedback time

Whether you are editing alone, or with an editor or choreographer, or as a three-person team, there comes a point at which other people – that is, those not directly involved in the editing process – will view the edit with the purpose of giving you feedback.

Exposing your work to a wider public, even if this is just one or two people, is a nerve-wracking experience. Editing is an intense job, demanding great amounts of personal, creative input from those involved. It can be unsettling, even painful, when someone new comes into this process, especially if they turn out to be in any way critical. But it can also be extremely helpful.

In a situation where a video dance work has been commissioned by a broadcaster or funding body, there will usually be one or more commissioning editors or executive producers overseeing all the productions. Try not to see them as the enemy, but instead, see them as the ultimate supporters of your project, who took it on board even when it was just an idea on paper.

Most on-the-ball executive producers will have kept in touch with the project's progress and may have even visited the shoot. Now they will want to view your off-line edit and will give their comments and feedback on it.

Having been involved in the project from so early on, the executive producers should know what your intention is for the work and will be sympathetic to your aims and ideals. They will ideally also be experienced in giving feedback, understanding the difference between being constructive and destructive at what can often be a sensitive time.

Tip!

Always set your computer to 'save as you go'. Although a bit irritating when it starts saving just as you want to do something, it is worth it to make sure that your work is being saved at regular intervals.

If your production has no 'bosses of the bosses', then it can be a good idea to invite one or two individuals whose opinions on video dance you trust to give you some feedback on your edit so far.

People who are really good at giving feedback are those who are able to see beyond their own personal tastes to what the intention of the work is and to assess if these intentions are being met. If they find the work lacking or confusing, they are able to describe why they feel this might be. You cannot necessarily expect them, or you might not want them, to offer exact solutions, but there is nothing more frustrating than someone saying that they do not think your edit is working, but they are not sure why!

If you have choice in the matter, consider with care at what point in the editing process external feedback is most useful and from whom.

Don't opt for feedback too soon. You do not want to have to explain everything and describe what is missing: it is better to let the work speak for itself, and this might be necessary if too little of the edit is in place. Also, feedback given too early can disrupt you and your collaborators own creative processes in the edit.

On the other hand, if you want to be able to act on other people's comments, then you must leave enough editing time after you have received the feedback to do so. Therefore, do not leave a viewing session until the very last day of your edit.

Before the actual viewing – and this goes for any feedback – rather than feel nervous, try and think what it is that you would like to know about the work as it stands now. If there are areas that you feel are still unresolved, ask direct questions from whoever has viewed the work and from the answers, try and work out if your fears are founded or not. Whilst you don't want to create work 'by committee', the opinions of a select few can be extremely helpful at this stage and can push your video dance from being 'OK' to absolutely brilliant!

If you find yourself in the situation that you disagree with the feedback that you are given, first of all take some time to reflect and think whether you are just feeling precious about something that you are very close to. Check that the work is as clear as you intend it to be.

On very rare occasions, there can be disagreements about the final version of an edit. When this is between yourself (and your team) and a commissioning editor of funder, then stick to your guns. Your individuality as an artist and as part of as a collaborative creative team is dependent on your unique view of the world and a particular approach to making art. Whilst in the commercial world it may be usual to have to act on the opinions of those who are paying for the work, in the creation of art, this is an unacceptable situation.

If the disagreement is between you and a close collaborator, say the choreographer or the producer, then this is when you need to have been very clear about who has the final say and, as we have already discussed, it is usually the director. The best approach of all is to avoid these conflicts by making sure that you are all working towards the same vision and to respect each other's input into the work.

Locking picture

At some point in the off-line, you need to stop making changes to the edit and move onto the next stage. Even if you have made a realistic assessment of how long you need to off-line your video dance, and if the shoot and the edit have gone smoothly, you will still probably feel as if you could do with more time. This is both natural and common.

Be reassured, however, that whilst you probably could go on editing your video dance for months and months, it would not necessarily be any better for it. Trust that the decisions that have been made in the time you have had are the right ones and look forward to the next part of the process.

Finalising the off-line edit in readiness for the on-line and then the sound dub is often referred to as 'locking picture'. This implies that there will be no changes to the visual structure of your work after this point. Nevertheless, as we will see in the next and final chapter of this book, the on-line and sound-dub stage of the process can radically alter the nature and experience of your video dance.

Having locked picture, the last technical task in the off-line is the creation of an 'edit decision list'. Generated by the editing software, this is all the data required to reconstruct your video dance as it was in its final version in the off-line.

Tip!

In some
situations, the
executive
producers ask to
'sign off' the
completed off-
line before it goes
on to the on-line
stage. If this is
the case, you will
need to schedule
time between the
end of the off-line
and the on-line.

When you go to the on-line, you will take your edit decision list, as well as all the rushes. These will be taken into the on-line editing system, ready to start work.

It is also essential to lay off a copy of your video dance onto tape, so that the on-line editor can check that what is assembled in the on-line is the same as the off-line.

Exercises

These exercises require a digital editing system and some video dance, with picture and audio. You can use the footage for the exercises from earlier chapters, if you did those.

Cuts, dissolves and micro-editing

For this exercise, you can use the footage that you shot for the 'In-camera montage' exercise in Chapter 2.

- Digitise material into your edit system.
- Select the clip that was the first shot in your montage exercise and place it onto the time-line. Decide if it needs some trimming to tidy it up, for example, if there is superfluous footage at the beginning or end of the shot.
- Now do the same with the second, third, fourth and fifth shot, until you have a short sequence of shots on the time-line.
- Now play this sequence and watch how the different shots work together. Does the sequence run fluidly between the shots of differ-ent sizes, or do some cuts seem to jump in an unpleasant way?
- Spend some time exploring how you can improve some of the edits, either by changing the order in which the shots come, or by altering the edits. Do this by losing a few frames from either the start of an incoming shot, or the end of an outgoing shot. Stick with cuts only.
- Once you are happy with your edited sequence, make a copy of it.
- Working on the copy, now try changing some or all of the edits into dissolves. Explore the difference between a very short dissolve and a longer fade between two shots.
- Compare your 'cut only' version and the one with dissolves.

Sound alternative

If you recorded audio with your pictures, then lay this down as synch sound with each clip. For the first part of the exercise, however, work with the sound muted. After a while, try what happens to your perception of the edited sequence when you also hear the synch sound. Now try by laying in music and notice how that changes things further.

Looping and repeating

- Select five short clips of video dance material. Name them A, B, C, D and E.
- Lay the first clip A on a time-line.
- Now repeat A ten times and watch back to see the effect:

  AAAAAAAAAA

- Copy this loop and lay it onto the original.

  AAAAAAAAAAAAAAAAAAAA

- Now take shot B and lay it in between the A shots of the second half of the sequence of twenty:

  AAAAAAAAAAABABABABABABABABABA

- Repeat this with all five shots so that you end up with a sequence like this:

  AAAAAAAAAAABABABABABABCABCABCABCABCABCACB
  ABCABCABCABCDABCDABCDABCDABCDABCDABCDABC
  DABCDABCDEABCDEABCDEABCDEABCDEABCDEABCDEA
  BCDE

- Now do the opposite, starting with the loop of all five shots, and gradually decreasing, like this:

  ABCDEABCDEABCDEABCDEABCDEABCDEABCDEABCDE
  ABCDABCDABCDABCDABCDABCDABCD
  ABCABCABCABCABCABCABC
  ABABABABABABABAB
  AAAAAAAA

This exercise can be evolved ad infinitum.

CONTENTS

CHAPTER 10

Final Stages

The final stages of post-production offer great opportunities to further enhance your video dance. The on-line is time to concentrate on the technical aspects of your edited visual material, to ensure that it is the best it can be.

Then it is time to shift the focus entirely to the soundtrack. Whilst audio should have been something that has been thought about since the very beginning of the process, it is now that this crucial element is shaped according to the needs of your video dance.

The on-line edit

An on-line can last between a few hours and a few days, depending on the length of your video dance and the complexity of what you need to achieve. If you take your project to a special high-end on-line suite, then you will most likely work with an on-line editor, who is trained to use that particular system.

As we saw at the end of the last chapter, the on-line system reads an edit-decision list that is generated in the off-line at the end of the editing period. This contains all the data needed to replicate exactly the structure that was created in the off-line. Using the original rushes from your shoot, the on-line system then recreates the off-line, this time at an extremely high technical level.

In the on-line, you concentrate entirely on the pictures. Sound comes later, in the dub. Now you will do 'for real' any effects that may have been incorporated in the off-line edit (for example, slow motion) and add some that were not possible in the off-line, depending on what software you were using and what equipment was available.

The on-line is where you can do colour alteration and corrections, and any on-screen text, such as the titles and credits, are created and added.

At the end of the on-line, the images of your video dance will be laid onto a high-quality format tape that becomes your master tape: the original version of your work from which all future copies will be made.

Colour correction

Once your video dance is reassembled in the on-line system, the next stage is to work on the colour of each individual clip.

Colour correction is the term used to describe any alteration you make to the colour of your edited material.

Sometimes it can be useful to have already made some alterations in the off-line – for example, if the colour of the image is greatly affecting the experience of different images being cut together. In general, however, there is not much point in doing any real work on colour until the on-line, for this is where you are creating the actual video images that will be laid down as your master tape.

Depending on the capabilities of the system that you are using for the on-line edit, there is much that you can do to affect the colour of the images.

- You can strip out or add in colour, making images bluer, pinker, less green and so on.
- If all the colour is taken away, your image becomes black and white, which is a popular effect.

The colour of each individual clip in your edit has a great impact on the way that the work will be perceived. As we saw in Chapter 4, specific post-production effects such as making some or all of your images into black and white, or giving them a very distinctive colour or tonal quality may have been part of your design plan.

The colour of each clip can also be adjusted to make whatever is featured in the frame seem more 'normal', and although these changes may be subtle, they will positively affect the viewers' experience of watching your work. You may notice, for example, that a certain light has made your performers' skin seem rather green. Skilful correction can restore them to a healthier colour!

Colour correction is usually carried out before any on-screen text is added, as the adding or the stripping away of colour will affect everything in the frame.

What's in a name? Adding a title and credits

Finding the right title for your video dance is extremely important.

At the beginning of the process, the title can help to define or clarify the idea that you are working with.

When the work is nearing completion, you need to reconsider and decide if the title you have is the still the best one for the work. It may be that the video dance has evolved into something rather different from what it started out as, and so its original, or 'working', title may no longer be suitable.

A well-chosen title can:

- intrigue
- invite
- suggest
- amuse
- explain, or
- pose a question to be answered.

Ideally, your chosen title should both look good on the page and sound good when spoken.

It is useful and enlightening to skim through the programmes of video dance festivals and read all the different titles that people choose for their work. Even if you haven't seen the actual video dance, you can tell that some titles are descriptive, others are oblique and some are very direct.

Once your title has been decided for definite, you must consider how it is going to appear in the edited video dance and what it will look like. Here are some things to think about.

- Is the title the first thing that the viewer will see, or will it appear after some moments or after some other credits?
- Will it be on black or against other images, either still or moving?
- Are you going to create a special title sequence for your video dance? If so, who will design this?

If you are short of ideas, watch already existing video dance works to see what solutions for titles other artists have come up with already. However, whilst it is great to be inventive, remember, the most important thing is that the title is clear and easy to read on screen. And it shouldn't look as if you've tried too hard.

Most on-line edit systems have graphic packages. Designing on-screen titles may be an area that your editor has skill in and he or she can create something in the edit. Alternatively, you can go all out and commission a special title sequence. Of course, this will cost money, so you need to be sure that it is necessary and that you have the budget available.

As in the movies and on most television programmes, it is convention to have credits on a video dance. The idea is that you let the viewer know who has fulfilled what role on the production.

In most video dance, the credits are placed at the end of the work. However, sometimes people like to have some names up front, at the beginning of the video dance, along with the title. Typically, these are the names of the main collaborators: the choreographer, director and dancers. Some people think that this is a good idea, as it lets people know whose work they are watching before they start. This is possibly of particular of interest especially if it is a name or names that they might know.

In general, on-screen credits that come at the end include:

- everyone who has worked on the production
- names (and logos) of funders, sponsors and in-kind supporters of the project
- the name of the production company or companies
- the name of the copyright holder
- the year in which the video dance was completed.

The priority with credits, as with the title, is that they are clear and easy to read. Choose the font carefully and look at whether they are white on black (usually clearest), black on white, or any other colour or against a colour or moving picture background.

You can have the credits moving across the screen, either 'scrolling' vertically or 'crawling' horizontally.

Don't be tempted to have any on-screen text appear, and then disappear too quickly. If you want people to be able to read the credits (and why have them if you don't?), then you have to allow enough time. A rule of thumb is that you should be able to read any on-screen text twice through. On the other hand, there is nothing worse than a never-ending list of credits crawling past too slowly, so don't be afraid to speed them up a bit if they feel laboured.

It is often best to compile the credits on your word processor before transferring the list to the on-edit system when it is complete.

Make sure that nobody who should be credited is missed out.

Check what people are happy to be called (e.g. Kathy or Katherine?). You should have agreed their title (Art Director or Production Designer) at the stage of issuing contracts and confirming bookings.

Check (and double-check) all on-screen spelling. There is nothing more likely to spoil the impression of your work than a wrongly spelt word or to annoy a collaborator than a typo in their name. As a fail-safe, ask someone else to spellcheck your credits list before it goes onto tape.

It is up to you to decide on the order in which the credits come. Be aware that broadcasters and commissioning bodies often have strict guidelines on these matters. These may cover who is named and the specific wording of credits, as well as their order and overall duration. Make sure you are clear about any requirements before your credits are finalised.

If your work is funded, then you will most likely need to credit whoever gave the money. They usually require not only a name credit, but also a logo. These are usually provided in a format that you can take into the on-line edit system, either downloaded off the web or direct from tape.

When designing your titles, make sure that they are within what is referred to as 'title safe'. Many televisions and monitors do not allow the viewer to see the entire rectangle of the video frame as it is in camera, losing up to a couple of centimetres from all around the image. An on-line edit system is equipped with a high-quality monitor with markings on that indicates which part of the screen is within title safe. As long as the text on your images is placed within these confines, they should be visible on any screen.

Producing a master tape

Having added your credits and titles and done any necessary colour correction, it is now time to lay your edited video dance onto a high-quality tape. This will be what is referred to as the 'master tape'.

When it is complete – that is, when the final mixed soundtrack is laid onto it and any picture grading is done – this master tape will be the version of the work from which all copies will be made. The most important things about the master is that it should never be used for the broadcast or screening of your work. Always use a copy. In these days of digital transfers, the quality difference need not even be noticeable.

You will also need at least two safety copies, of equal quality to the master, and these should be stored separately from the master, and also not used for screenings.

If your work is the result of a co-production or core collaboration, then each party may want to have their own high-quality copy of the work, from which they too can make copies.

Finally, double-check what format is required for delivery to any broadcasters or funding organisation that commissioned your work. They will have stipulated what they require and, again, this should be a high-quality copy and not one of your master tapes.

Tip!

Invest in a fire- and waterproof box for storing your master tapes and have a safety one or two stored separately, ideally in different locations in case of fire.

Creating your soundtrack

'Sound is the most visceral element in film; in other words, if you want to get the audience in the gut, it's the sound that gets them, not the images. On film, you can take the tiniest of all breaths, that not even the first row in the theatre would hear, and make it into an extraordinarily powerful element. If that helps with the meaning of what you are trying to get across, then take that breath and use it.'

David Hinton, director

Sound is highly evocative. It opens up the imagination. Where a picture shows you how things are, sound suggests many different possibilities of how things might be.

When you are creating the soundtrack for your video dance, you will be working with:

- rhythm
- texture
- tone
- volume
- space
- movement
- density and sparseness, and
- silence.

Whatever the nature of your video dance and the kind of soundtrack that you want, you must remember that you are not stuck with the way things are in real time and space. The potential is much greater if you think about it only in relation to how the visual and aural images of your video dance relate to and affect each other.

Although your soundtrack does not have to be complex, it will probably be made up of layers, including different elements such as:

- music
- actuality sound recorded on the shoot
- sound effects created in the studio.

How these are selected, combined, edited, mixed and juxtaposed with the visual images is the art of creating a soundtrack and has the potential to add many layers of meaning and richness to your video dance work.

Working with music

Music can be a wonderful addition to your video dance. It can add atmosphere and mood, pace and drama. It can evoke different times, places and seasons.

As we have seen previously, music can become part of the video dance-making process at different stages.

- It can be used to provide the stimulus and the structure for the choreography of the dancers.
- It can be used as the structural basis for some, or all, of the off-line editing.
- It can be composed, recorded and added towards the end of the process, at the final sound dub.

The styles of music that can be used are limitless, and it can be fascinating to explore the effect that different types of music have on the edited video dance.

However, using music in a video dance soundtrack can also be problematic. For example, either the music seems too dominant, forcing the visual images to recede, or the music has become too bland, and it just disappears into the background.

Sometimes there just seems to be a conflict, as if there is just not room for the melodies and rhythms of most music to co-exist, let alone work with, the visual rhythms of video dance.

Rhythm is key to understanding how music works with edited video dance. You have the rhythms of the choreography, the rhythms of the camera movement and the rhythms of the editing. What's more, it is also likely that you will also want to use other sounds, such as synch and effects, to enhance your soundtrack.

The problems often arise when you then lay music on top of these already existing layers of rhythm and it takes great skill to compose – or to find – music that can work with, rather than against, these different elements.

Of course, where the filming and editing has been based on the music and its relationship to choreography, then this should not be a problem. The challenge comes when the structure of the video dance is being determined by other factors. This is why it is so important to work with a composer or soundtrack designer who understands both your vision for your work and the nature of video dance.

'In drama, you are usually dealing with a strong narrative that is dialogue-led. If you are using a piece of music in the soundtrack, you don't want it to have a melody, because then you will have two melodies: you've got the musical melody and the melody of speech in the dialogue, and what the audience is trying to do is to follow two trains of thought at the same time, which can be difficult. It's the same with dance film, except that you have a visual rhythm rather than dialogue.'

John Cobban, sound designer/dubbing mixer

Actuality sound

As we have seen, in video dance, the actuality sounds are usually the noises made by the performers' feet on the surface of the floor, or by their bodies moving against each other, or another object, as well as the sound of their breath.

These actuality sounds can be 'synch sounds' because they are synchronised with the visual image of the action that is creating the noise, or they can also be recorded as 'wild-tracks', which means that the audio is not attached to a particular visual image.

Actuality sounds are very useful in video dance soundtracks. Very often, they are mixed in with music to add a liveness – and a liveliness – to the soundtrack. Without these sounds, the images and the sounds can feel very disconnected and the dance itself can come across flat and undynamic.

'Having the synch sound, that is your bottom level. If you don't, you're into silent-movie territory. Once you've got the synch sound there, then you can start playing and either make things "hyper", or almost cartoon-like, so that people are really aware of sound and it's a real feature. Or if you do not want to go that far, you can just enhance the movement through sound and make it look a lot sharper, a lot more in time and more musical.'

Billy Cowie, director/choreographer

Beyond using them in this more conventional way, sounds recorded on the shoot can form the basis of your soundtrack.

This is an approach that I have taken in many of the video dance works that I have directed and, for me, it can provide a very effective starting point for the creation of an evocative, multi-layered soundtrack. In some of my more recent work, the entire soundtrack has been made up simply of sounds from the shoot, and yet if you watch and listen to the work, you would not guess that the source of the 'music' is so simple.

The process begins with ensuring that we record as high-quality synch sound as possible on the shoot.

As I am viewing and selecting the material that I want to take into the edit, I log takes that have particularly interesting audio, as well as any wild-tracks that may have been recorded.

Then, in the off-line, we tend simply to leave the synch sound attached to the different clips with which we are working and see – and hear – what happens as the images are juxtaposed and looped during the visual editing process. We may also lay in some wild-tracks or shift some of the synch sound around (there is nothing to say that a sound needs to stay with its related visual image).

When the off-line is complete, and the picture locked, sound designer John Cobban and I work together to build up a soundtrack, based on this original actuality sounds.

The creative work that John does usually involves his trawling through all the rushes, listening to everything that was recorded. For him, this process involves identifying small moments that represent the essence of the work or evoke a particular mood or energy.

Gradually, he builds a palette of audio material that can be used in his soundtrack edit.

Then, often taking as his starting point the structure provided by the synch sound that was left in place in the off-line, he will begin to evolve an overall structure for the soundtrack. This may involve looping short clips, juxtaposing different sections of sound and adding layers and pads of sound.

This is intensive work and it can take several days to compose the sound-track of a ten-minute long video dance. I find it an incredibly effective way of working, in which the soundtrack that is created becomes music, not as in a sequence of notes, but like a shifting and evocative landscape.

Additional sound recording

As well as working with the actuality sound recorded on the shoot, you have the possibility to source any other sounds to involve in your soundtrack.

The common practice in feature films is that all the sound – even the dialogue – is recorded in a sound studio at a later date. Any sound recorded on the shoot is for guide only.

Whilst you are not necessarily dealing with dialogue, it is good to keep this image in your head as it helps with the concept of creating a soundtrack that is separate to what happened in 'real' life and will encourage you to think creatively and ambitiously about the use of sound in your video dance.

A very creative way to work is to create your soundtrack mainly, or entirely, with specially recorded sounds. Working in a sound-recording studio, you can create any sounds and effects that you desire from scratch. This recording is called 'foley'.

You can simply recreate movements and record their sounds, or you can let your imagination and creativity loose and conjure up all sort of different aural effects using anything and everything that makes the noise you are looking for.

'After the film is shot and edited, we go into the sound studio and I get into a small box and reperform the piece whilst watching it on the monitor. I make sounds as close to what I did as I can and Billy (Cowie) can then work them back into the soundtrack. We both raid our houses for things that make good noises, and then spend a lot of time throwing things around in the sound booth, generating other sounds, that are then also added into the soundtrack.'

Liz Aggiss, director/choreographer

Editing the soundtrack

The most important thing about your soundtrack is that it is working to compliment and enhance the visual images.

Sounds can exaggerate and be unreal. They can compliment and contradict.

As sound is so evocative, what you choose to work with can add a whole new layer of meaning to an image.

The way that the sound is effected can impact on the sense of space that is created by an image. In Chapter 7, we looked at different ways of recording sound on the shoot, and the importance of having good, clean, close-up actuality sound. With this in place, a sound designer can add different effects and processes to the audio, altering what the sound communicates about the action and the space in which it is happening.

Using a sound-editing system, the soundtrack designer can cut and paste clips of audio in a similar way to what happens in the picture edit. The big difference is here that he or she can work to much greater detail, making alterations of hundredths of a second.

Dubbing and mixing

The sound dub is where the final structure of your soundtrack is created.

It's essential that any audio elements that need to be pre-recorded, such as the music, are then complete before this next stage in the process begins.

Depending on the way that whoever is creating your overall soundtrack wants to work, any additional sound recording may also need to be complete. Otherwise they may be done as the soundtrack is designed.

The next stage is that all the different elements are taken into the system and then laid down on the audio time-line. Usually, the director works closely with the sound designer in the dub. This is a creative process rather like the off-line edit, in which decisions are made about rhythm, structure, flow and timing.

When everything is in place, an audio time-line might look something like Figure 10.1, showing the various layers of audio in relation to the edited pictures.

Once everything is in position, it's time for the mix to happen. This is where the balance between the different layers of sound is created and the final soundtrack is laid down onto the master tape.

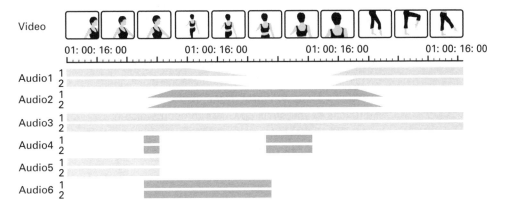

Figure 10.1 An audio timeline

The relationship between the many layers of sounds is crucial, and the skill of a good dubbing mixer is to create the right balance between all the elements that have been incorporated in the sound edit.

It is important to listen back to the mix-down versions several times, checking whether the relative strengths of the different sounds are how you want them. Be aware that listening through the high-quality speakers in the suite does not represent how most people will hear the work. Instead, try out what the mix sounds like played through some television speakers (that's the most common way the work will be heard). Similarly, it is useful to make a copy of the work and to have a look and listen at home, before returning to the dub to make any final adjustments. The overall effect of the soundtrack can feel very different when taken out of the dubbing-suite context.

The volume of the soundtrack is taken from the relative levels of the different layers of sounds within your soundtrack. An experienced sound designer or dubbing mixer will know the correct level for the soundtrack according to the standards set for cinema screenings and for broadcast.

Laying off

When the mixing is complete, it is time for the soundtrack to be laid off onto your master tape.

It can be useful to have different mixes of your soundtrack for different purposes. You can do this on a high-quality copy of the master, or sometimes even on extra audio channels on the master tape itself.

With many of the video dance works that I have directed, we have had both a 'cinema mix' and a 'television mix'. This has enabled us to push certain aspects of the mix in the knowledge that a cinema sound system would cope with it, whilst at the same time, to compensate for the limitations of the small speakers through which most people would watch the work at home or in a video dance library booth. If you take this approach, be sure that your different masters with the alternative mixes are clearly labelled.

C O N T E N T S

CHAPTER 11

Out on the Road

It is often with a great sense of relief that you walk away from the sound dub, master tape in hand, your long-awaited video dance ready to be seen by the world.

But now a new type of journey begins: that of the work out into the world. How it is received depends not just on the effort and artistry so far, but also on the imagination and energy that you are prepared to put into its presentation and distribution.

Getting your work seen

With the making of your video dance finally complete, it is time to turn your attention to how and where it is going to be viewed.

If you are in the position of having had the work commissioned, it is likely that it will be screened or broadcast as part of a series or scheme. However, even if this involves a number of public outings for your video dance, it is more than likely that you will want to seek out further opportunities for your work to be seen, worldwide and locally.

Remember, it is not necessarily a given that what you have made must be released out into the world for anyone to see. As we saw in Chapter 1, it may be that the priority of your project was to experiment with some new ideas or to gain experience.

Now that the work is completed, you may feel that, whilst it has fulfilled its intention, the resulting video dance may not be good enough to be seen by a wider audience. Remember, if you want to involve yourself in raising funds for future work, then you must be careful about what people see of your work.

'In terms of getting commissions, by far the most important thing is doing good work, because a huge amount of it is about them trusting you on the basis of what you have done before. If you have done good stuff then the commissioning people have in their heads that this is somebody who they can trust. It also means it's very, very dangerous to do bad stuff, because they will say: "Oh he's gone off." It's impossible for people to judge the idea independently from the people who are going to be making it.'

David Hinton, director

The best way to find out about opportunities to have your video dance seen by the public is to get onto the Internet and to do your research. The web sites listed in the Resources section at the end of this book are a good place to start.

The most usual outlets for video dance are:

- festivals

- television
- cinemas and theatres
- on-line.

There are a few companies that distribute short films. Whilst most of these are regular, dialogue-based work, some video dance works do slip through the net and find their way onto the books. However, the main focus of these distributors usually seems to be selling shorts to television companies. The work of getting video dance into festivals and onto cinema screens almost always comes down to the artist.

Festivals

It seems like every year a new festival is added to the international video dance calendar. The number and range of these festivals indicates that there is a growing public interest in dance made for the screen, and an ever-increasing number of people producing video dance all over the world.

Festivals are the main outlet for video dance, and you need to know about them if you want to get your work seen.

Video dance festivals come in all different shapes and sizes. Most of them have web sites, and this is the best way to find out about the character and remit of a particular festival.

There are many general short-film festivals all over the world, some of which may accept and screen video dance. Again, information about these can be found on-line.

Some festivals have open submissions, which mean you can send your work in, with the appropriate application form, all requested information and, usually, an entrance fee.

Some festivals accept all work that is submitted. Others are selective and they comprise of specially curated screenings, usually based on a theme or type. For example, programmes might be of 'New Hungarian Video Dance' or have a title like 'Bodies in the Frame'.

Some festivals run competitions ('Best Screen Choreography', Best New Hungarian Production', etc.). Whilst you do not make work to win prizes, if your work does pick up an award, it can make a huge difference to the life of the work and to your chances of securing funding for future projects.

As well as sending your work out to festivals, it's a great idea to attend them. Many video dance festivals programme panel discussions with practitioners and other key professionals, or they set up 'meet the commissioner' sessions or pitching competitions. All these events can be an excellent way of extending your knowledge of the art form as well as alerting you to funding and screening opportunities.

Festivals are also the best place to watch work (you can often view all the festival submissions in the festival library), and are an excellent way to meet fellow artists and interested audiences.

If your own video dance work is in a festival, then all the more reason to attend, as you can provide some 'on-site' publicity, handing out postcards detailing any special screenings of your work.

A very few festivals invite key production personnel (usually the director, producer or choreographer) to come and introduce their work. Such opportunities are really worth taking up; it is a great way to receive feedback on your video dance, and audiences really appreciate hearing artists talk about their work.

'When you are sending your dance film out, you should try and educate yourself about differences in the festivals. For example, not all of them show the work on big screen, some just have video libraries where people can view the work. And be strategic. Look at a festival's past programming and assess how your work might fit in, then you maybe don't need to send out so many tapes.'

Erin Brannigan, curator

Unfortunately, not all festivals are good festivals. A few are so disorganised that you have to consider carefully whether is worth the considerable time and effort it takes to send your video dance in and, importantly, if it is the context in which you wish your work to be seen.

Checking out the web site and seeing what other work has been screened there in the past can be a good way of assessing the status of a festival. Or ask other artists to see what experience they have had of a particular festival or organisation.

Television

Unless a broadcaster commissioned your video dance, it is extremely difficult to have it screened on television. Opportunities to schedule dance on television are very rare, and programmes that the broadcaster has already paid for usually must fill any slots. However, there is the odd exception, and if you feel that your work is suitable for television, this is a potentially exciting area to explore.

Whilst the main terrestrial channels may have limited openings for video dance, some of the cable and digital channels are more flexible in what they can programme.

In feature films and even short narrative films, the conventional way to approach television channels is through a sales agent. However, I am not sure that there are many who would tackle such a specialist area as video dance. In a sense, this works in your favour, for if you do attend festivals, you are quite likely to come across the actual executive producer or programme buyer of a channel's art or dance programme and you can make a direct approach to them about screening your video dance.

The other way to do it is to find out who programmes dance at a particular channel and to simply send him or her a viewing copy, along with a letter of introduction.

Cinemas and theatres

Some cinemas programme short films in front of feature films, and this can be a lovely way of having your work reach an audience that might not go to a specialist video dance festival.

There are some agencies that set up these opportunities, but with your local cinema, often the best way is to make contact with the programmer or manager and ask them if they would be interested in viewing your work, with a view to screening it. If you are lucky, they may be inspired to schedule it alongside a musical matinee or whatever other film they feel it complements.

Another way forward is to suggest a programme of video dance at the cinema. I have often found that there is a great enthusiasm and interest in video dance, just not that much information about the work that is already out there. Maybe you can help curate a mini-festival and thereby helping to build new audiences for video dance.

Text to go with work

Your work has been created for others to see, and a large part of making this happen is to entice people to watch it. The text that accompanies your video dance – and how it is presented – plays an important part in this. Wherever your work is to be seen, it will need some kind of written introduction to accompany it. This might be included in a festival brochure, on the back of a postcard advertising your film, announced on a television programme or on a web site.

You cannot depend on the fact that the viewer will necessarily read the text before they see your work, but if they do, you must decide what you would like them to know.

As when you wrote your treatment early on in the process, the style and content of your text is up to you. As then, your approach to writing may reflect the nature of the video dance.

It is useful to prepare texts of different lengths. Sometimes all that is required is a few sentences, whereas other times there is space and a demand for more detail about the work and its creators. It is useful to store several different versions of the text on your personal computer, to call up whenever you need them.

'The accompanying text that is sent in with most dance films is usually pretty bad and has to be to be rewritten for the festival programme. But I don't mind this, as for me, the programme notes describe the curatorial ideas and themes of the festival. Too often, the text I receive reads very blandly, like: "This is an exploration of . . . whatever". They are too open and don't really say anything. So, try and really think what makes your film different from the rest and, if you can't think what makes your film different, then maybe you have to look at what it is that you are making!'

Erin Brannigan, curator

Along with the text about the video dance work, you will often need biographical information about the key creative collaborators on the project. It is a good idea to write this text up towards the end of the post-production process, so that it is ready and waiting for when you need it. The longer you leave it, the harder it will be to make contact with everyone whose information you need, as they will be onto new projects.

If the video dance has a long life, it is a good idea to update the biographical information, so that it is as relevant as possible and so that you do not miss out on any exciting developments that might reflect positively on your own video dance (one of your dancers might have become a Hollywood star!).

It is also a good idea to regularly refresh any text about the video dance. As the work does the rounds, you will want to add information about significant screenings or any awards or reviews that it receives.

Photographs

Essential for any publicity for your video dance are some good quality photographs. The video dance works that have a high profile on the festival scene are inevitably the ones that provided a striking photographic image.

Ideally, you might have had a photographer on your shoot, and you can also create some digital stills from your completed video dance. Between the two types of photographs, select around six images that will become the ones that are used in all the publicity surrounding your work.

It is useful to store these photos as digital images on your computer, so that they can be e-mailed immediately as they are needed with the minimum of fuss. They should be the best quality possible, especially if they are to be reproduced for print.

Tip!

Insist that photos are credited when used. Ideally, the name of the photographer, production and dancers featured should be included.

'A good image can really swing things for you, because, if you have a wonderful photo to go with your film and the film is on the cusp of being in or out of a festival, the fact that there is this great image that can be used for the marketing of the festival may mean that the film gets selected.'

Erin Brannigan, curator

Packaging and boxes

Getting your video dance seen always involves sending off viewing copies of the work and, trivial though it may seem, it is worth thinking about the packaging.

Whatever the format of the copies, it is a good idea to have a plastic or cardboard cover. It will protect the copy from dust and damage, and it is also an opportunity to include texts and eye-catching photographic images.

If graphic design is not your strong point, ask somebody to do the job for you. It is certainly worth making a bit of an effort with the presentation, as the packaging of your video dance is likely to be the first aspect of your work that any prospective curators or broadcasters comes across.

Your video dance web site

The Internet is increasingly being used as the place to research, exchange information about and even view video dance work.

You can have a web site specifically for an individual work, or you can build up a portfolio web site, which includes information about all the work you have made (an example of this can be found at www.left-luggage.co.uk).

A web site relating to an individual work might include:

- text about the video dance work detailing any broadcast, festival screenings or awards that it has had to date
- photos – stills from the video dance and from the shoot
- biographical information about the creative team
- video clips with scenes from your work or the entire work
- your contact details and information about how the work can be obtained for screenings or bought for libraries or personal collections.

Take as much care with the design and construction of your web site as you do with your video dance work, as it might be someone's first introduction to your work.

It's essential to let people know about your web site. Compile a list of interested people and e-mail them to let them know about the site. You can do regular updates, with information about upcoming screening and so on, but be sure to follow Internet etiquette and respect any requests to be taken off your mailing list.

The beauty of a web site is that, if regularly added to, it can evolve into an archive and a valuable resource, for yourself and anyone interested in your work.

Experiencing your work

It is inevitably going to be strange experience, watching your video dance 'going public' for the first time. Especially as the post-production stages of the work usually involve only two or three people working closely together over several weeks, it can be a shock to the system to be showing your work to people who are not intimately involved in its creation.

I am not sure which is more scary: a large-scale screening in a cinema, or showing your work to one or two people, on a small screen in a cramped space. Here are some suggestions on how to survive either – or both – of these experiences.

- Never make excuses for your work. If you and your team have worked hard and with integrity, then you should be proud of what you have achieved.
- Be very careful not to (publicly) apportion blame for aspects of the production that you consider not to have been successful. Remember, as the director, you have ultimate control and vision and therefore are responsible for ensuring that the completed work is as close to your vision as possible. This does not mean that there will not be something about the completed work that you might not be happy about. I can't imagine anyone honestly sitting back and saying to themselves: 'I've just created the perfect video dance.' Be honest but philosophical about any shortcomings.
- Listen to the thoughts of others on your work, but do not take everything to heart.

It is very difficult to view your work with a critical eye, and yet this is something that you should attempt to do in the weeks, months and even years after the work is complete.

Try to experience your own work in different situations: watch it when it is broadcast on television, go to as many public screenings as you can and view it on your monitor at home. It continually amazes me how much a video dance can change, depending on the context, although nothing physical is actually altered (apart, perhaps, from the quality of the actual screening).

Discuss the successes and failures of the work with your collaborators; see if there are aspects that you all might have done differently, had you known, and acknowledge the things that worked really well.

The next step

Making video dance can be very hard, and at various points in the production process, you may think to yourself 'Never again!'. That is natural, but it is also likely that, with the premiere screening behind you, a few nice comments from your friends and family (and even other artists and professionals), and some rest and recuperation, you may eventually feel like making another video dance work.

In the world of narrative-fiction film-making, shorts are often considered to be a stepping stone towards producing or directing feature films. In video dance, this is less likely – it is hard enough to find the resources to make a 10-minute-long video dance, let alone fund one of 90-plus minutes. In any case, there are only very few examples of that length, so it is really hard to gauge how well video dance works over that duration and, most importantly, where the audience for feature-length video dance would be found.

It is much more likely that you will go on to to make another short video dance work. Hopefully, what you have read in this book will have helped you through the process to date and will inspire you in the future. To conclude, I'd like to leave you with some thoughts, or suggestions.

- Look for any opportunities for making new video dance, but if none come up, then create your own.

- It's OK (in fact, very good) to keep exploring the same or similar themes and ideas in your work, but don't repeat yourself. Look for new images, new sounds, new forms and new ways of working.
- Keep watching other artists' work, but don't be swayed from your own vision. If you feel that you are swimming against the tide, examine what you are trying to do, but do not necessarily change direction.
- Look for chances to collaborate with artists from all backgrounds who offer another perspective on creating work; it makes for an exciting, stimulating, productive, if not an easy life.
- Remember, the video dance you are making is the most important thing in the world – and the least important thing in the world. Care about what you are doing. Be diligent, careful, hard-working. Treat the work and your collaborators with respect and honour. But don't let your work rule or ruin your life and bear in mind that you are not saving lives, so don't take your work – or yourself – too seriously.

CONTENTS

Production credits

Kate Gowar: dancer/commissioner and co-producer

Karin Fisher-Potisk: dancer/commissioner and co-producer

Simon Fildes: editor and co-producer

Katrina McPherson: director and co-producer

Paulo Ribeiro: choreographer

Fin Walker: choreographer

Rob Tannion: dancer

Matthew Morris: dancer

Neville Kidd: lighting cameraman

Ben Park: composer

Tracey Holder: production co-ordinator

Jo Holding: production manager

Fernando Mialski: costume designer

Miranda Melville: production designer

Gill Clark: performance advisor

Sarah Dowling: runner

Jono Smith: lighting cameraperson

Amy Holly: runner

Zarina Yeoh: runner

Arun Taylor: grip

Jason Clare: camera assistant

Ian Currie: sound recordist

Katherine Grincell: colourist

John Cobban: dubbing mixer

CHAPTER 12

Diary

The Making of *The Truth*, a half-hour video dance

This is the diary kept by Katrina McPherson, director and co-producer of *The Truth*, throughout the production process.

March 2002

Kate and Karin of Ricochet Dance Productions approach Simon and myself to ask whether we would be interested in making a new work with them. We are and resolve that both companies will be available to go full-time on the project at the beginning of 2003. Decide to put all other discussions on hold until August, a few months after Simon and my first child is due to be born.

September 2002

Kate and Karin visit Simon and I at our home in the Highlands. Time for us to come up with an idea for the new video project. All very clear that we want to make a video dance that puts choreography and the dancers' performance at the heart of the work.

Proposal evolves to make a work that challenges the viewer to question their memory and understanding of what they have seen: i.e. What is the truth of a situation? This is inspired by our discussions about the widespread use of CCTV or surveillance images by the media and how these are exploited to develop speculative narratives around certain everyday events, which then become high profile and locked into the public's consciousness.

We decide that the video dance – working title 'In Truth' – will have two very different types of material. There will be CCTV-style images, which will be filmed in a public or semi-public environment, and dance sections, which will be filmed in an interior, or more stylised location. We anticipate that the movement in the CCTV images will be pedestrian and the dance sections will have highly developed choreography.

The idea is that there will be four characters who are followed through a series of interactions caught on CCTV. What happens in the 'dance sections' will then add to and colour our reading of the relationships between the four characters. Each time we return to the CCTV scenes, our perception of the four characters' relationships has been altered.

We are taking an unconventional approach as we plan to work with three choreographers, asking each to create a body of movement based on the starting point we give them, which is to explore the idea of 'the truth'. They will not be aware of where or how their material will be filmed, nor how it is to be edited, although they will give feedback on the edit. This is because we are interested in exploring what happens when the same information is interpreted by various individuals through the many layers of the creative process.

The other major topic of conversation at this point is the budget. Many unknowns at this stage, but we have decided that we want the technical quality to be as high as possible, so we will shoot on digi-beta format. After some calculations, we realise that working with three choreographers is out of the question financially, and so we decide to go with two.

October–December 2002

Choreographers Paulo Ribeiro from Portugal and Fin Walker from England have agreed to work on the project, which is very exciting. I know both of their work, but have not met either of them. They have very different styles, which will provide us with an excellent contrast.

Kate and Karin have also asked two very experienced male dancers, Rob Tannion and Matthew Morris, to work on the project, and they are available and willing.

Lots of toing and froing between us all devising a production plan, based on people's availability and how long we can afford to rehearse, shoot and edit. As yet there is no first screening date, but we are aiming to rehearsal January–February, shoot early March and have post-production complete by the end of April.

Wednesday 8 January 2003

Choreographer Paulo's first day in rehearsal. I meet him and dancers over lunch and we have a brief chat about the ideas for the work. Paulo says that he is keen to choreograph a series of quartets (we had suggested solos, duets and trios would be most useful). We agree that he should start creating movement first and that we'll talk about configurations at a later point.

Call lighting cameraman Neville Kidd to check his availability. We've worked together a lot in the past and I'd love for him to film *In Truth*, but we don't really have the budget to bring him and his team down to London (he's Glasgow-based). I am weighing up what we could do without to ensure that we can have him.

Thursday 9 January 2003

Spent the morning in the Film Commission location library researching possible locations. Found photographs and details about Bethnal Green Town Hall. It's grand, but a bit shabby and would seem to offer several very different spaces within the one location. I put in a call and find out that the commercial rate for hire is £2,000 per day, which immediately puts it beyond our budget. There may be room for negotiation, so I arrange to go and see it anyway.

Friday 10 January 2003

Spent an hour or so at the studio today.

Watched the dancers perform what Paulo has choreographed in the first three days: a solo for each of the dancers, then a quartet and two duets. It's very exciting to see how things are developing.

Paulo is exploring the idea of 'truth' by asking 'What is the truth?'. 'The truth is falling down', Paulo tells me. He is going to have each of his sections end with someone falling down.

Sunday 12 January 2003

Meeting with everyone involved in the production so far: Paulo and Fin, composer Ben Park, production co-ordinator Tracey Holder, production manager Jo Holding, Karin, Kate, Simon and myself. An excellent opportunity to all sit around one table to discuss our vision for the film.

Paulo and Fin are particularly interested to know if I plan to intercut their material or to create a 'film in two halves'? I am not sure yet, and they agree that either approach is acceptable to them.

Monday 13 January 2003

Scout a loft space in Clapham. Too small for what we are looking for.

Tuesday 14 January 2003

Simon and I go and look at Bethnal Green Town Hall. Take lots of photos. It has the look of a disused hotel, which was one of the early images we talked about. Seems as though we might be able to negotiate a cheaper deal for hire of the building, as it is not much in demand right now.

Also go to Waterloo Station. A great space, so light and airy. Standing on the mezzanine level, looking down at the hundreds of people moving across or waiting on the concourse, we realise that the station offers huge potential as the 'exterior/public' location for filming the CCTV images. The concourse floor is white with black parallel lines running across – the geometry would work really well in the frame.

Wednesday 15 January 2003

Meeting with composer Ben Park.

Ben talks about the kind of instruments he is thinking of working with: French horn, violin, electronically generated sounds and a rhythm section.

We agree that he should compose and record short sections of music rather than one continuous piece and that we'll have some rough versions of these to work with in the off-line.

Ben and I both watch a run-through of Paulo's material. I record a wide shot on video, so that I can watch the material at home as many times as I want. This will familiarise me with it and give me time to think about how it might be filmed.

Decide that Liverpool Street Station is perfect for our public space and I phone up the company that manages the station to ask permission.

Lots of thinking and long discussions with Kate, Karin and Simon about the location for the choreography/internal sections. Concerned that a very distinct space like Bethnal Green Town Hall might push the film in too narrative a direction. Also, the nineteenth-century/Victorian architecture might be strangely incongruous with the modern feel of Liverpool Street Station. We start to veer back towards the idea of the dance sections being filmed in an airy, bright loft/studio-type space.

We approach costume designer Fernando Mialski and Miranda Melville (Min), a production designer, both of whom have experience on video dance and theatre productions and ask them to work on the project. They both agree and it's a relief to know that they will now begin to contribute to ideas and practicalities of the look of the film.

Thursday 16 January 2003

Rehearsals with Paulo and the dancers.

Film with mini-DV camera. Go handheld, responding instinctively to what I see through the lens. Find myself drawn to close-ups that detail the choreography.

We look back at the material on a monitor in the studio. Paulo likes the duets and feels that they could be filmed even closer. Other sections he'd like wider because, he explains, the choreographic structure is very much about the detail moving though the whole body.

It's early days for me to decide how exactly the material will be filmed as a lot will depend on the location and overall structure of the work, which is still to be evolved. But it's very useful to hear Paulo's thoughts.

Make a call to another possible location we've heard about – some artists' studios in Dalston.

Friday 17 January 2003
Spent some more time filming in the studio with Paulo and the dancers.

I've been thinking about locations for the dance sections and realise that all the spaces we have looked at so far have had concrete floors. Discuss this with the dancers who say that, if it's essential from an aesthetic point of view, they will dance on a hard floor. We agree that the production should buy them all new trainers with thick soles.

Paulo leaves for Portugal, as it is the end of his two-week creation period. He's choreographed a lot of great material (around 12 minutes) with the four dancers – more than we'd anticipated.

Saturday 18 January 2003
Simon and I return to Liverpool Street station to do some research for the CCTV images. From up on the mezzanine, I film Simon walking around, sometimes stopping to loiter and look. Using my DV camera, I shoot from several different angles. These images give me plenty of ideas about how the dancers will look in the context of all the station activity.

We also go and see the Dalston location. It's a gallery space in an old factory. My initial feeling is that it is too small, but as we explore it, we begin to realise that it does offer some interesting possibilities.

There are a number of interconnected spaces of different sizes, all with white walls and pale grey floors (could be painted). There are bars overhead from which lights can be hung and plenty of electric sockets. The building apparently has a flat roof, so it might also be possible to light by shining a lamp through the skylights. Being able to get the lights up high may compensate for the tightness of the space. I film some DV footage of the space to show the others.

Tuesday 21 January 2003
With Paulo away and Fin not due to start rehearsals, there's time to work on the station/CCTV scenes. The dancers and I spent some time in the studio exploring some improvisations and scenarios. I show them the footage from the station, which gives them further ideas on which to base their actions.

Wednesday 22 January 2003
Found our perfect dance location today: the space owned by the Victoria Miro Gallery, right next door to their main exhibition hall. A large, empty warehouse: white walls, smaller spaces off, concrete floors, beautiful windows. The commercial rate for hiring it is way out of our league, but we may be able to work something out with the gallery owner. I feel euphoric after such a long search.

Then, big blow, when they check the diary and we realise that it is not free until Thursday 13 March, the day before dancer Rob is flying out to a job in Hong Kong, and a week later than we had planned to film. Feel gutted.

Although Paulo is now away, the dancers have been rehearsing. Today, dance artist Gill Clark comes and watches a run-through of all Paulo's choreography in the studio. She is going to act as an performance advisor – a kind of 'outside eye' on the movement during the filming as the choreographers won't be there. The dancers, Gill and I had a very useful conversation about the intention of the different sections of Paulo's choreography.

Thursday 23 January 2003
Work on 'Party' section. Try out what it's like when the camera moves in and around the dancers as though it was another dancer. Getting clearer ideas of how to film Paulo's material.

Friday 24 January 2003
Have come up with solution that may mean we can film in the lovely Miro space. If we shift all our filming days later, and shoot for three days instead of four, it may work out that we can do two days in the Dalston

space, followed by one long day at Miro. This not only fits in with the Miro availability, but shooting three instead of four days eases the budget and means that we can afford to pay for the big space. It will only work for us if we can set up at Miro overnight on Wednesday 12 March, ready to film from early on the Thursday. (Rob has agreed to this, despite having to fly across the world the following day.) I e-mail this proposed schedule to the gallery owner. We can only wait and hope.

Wednesday 30 January 2003

Kate and Karin look at two more location possibilities. They film some mini-DV footage, which they then send up to me.

Friday 31 January 2003

I look at the footage of the two other locations. Now that I have the Miro space in my mind, nothing else seems as perfect.

Thursday 6 February 2003

With the locations becoming clearer (although not confirmed), production designer Min and I have some discussions about the environment we are trying to create in the dance sections. Not domestic, more official, yet with personal effects – pictures of unknown people on the wall to suggest surveillance of some type.

Tuesday 11 February 2003

Sarah, one of our three runners, goes off to Dalston to recce cafés nearby to the locations, as neither have catering facilities. We are also looking for somewhere near the Dalston space in which the dancers can warm up and prepare, as there are no suitable spaces in the location itself.

Speak to Min about the different types of coverings that could be in the locations. We have the idea of strips of wallpaper that might identify a space, but might then disappear in the next shot. Another design angle on the 'What did I actually see?' theme.

Wednesday 12 February 2003

Receive an e-mail from Kathy Stephenson, head of Publicity and Events at Victoria Miro Gallery, saying that the gallery owner is happy to support our project by reducing the hire cost and accommodating our timetable needs. This is wonderful news.

We can now schedule the shoot, based on one day prep and two days filming at Dalston, then an overnight set-up, a long day filming and half a day clear-up at Miro. Three days filming is not going to be a lot of time, so my shot list is going to have to be extra well prepared.

Monday 17 February 2003

Fin's creation period starts. She has ten days in which to choreograph her material. She's seen nothing of what Paulo has done, and the dancers are asked not to discuss locations or costumes. I'm staying out of the way for the first few days to let them get going.

Thursday 20 February 2003

It's become clear that Neville is not going to be free to film and so I approach Jono Smith, an excellent, London-based lighting cameraperson with whom I have worked on a number of documentary programmes for television.

Jono is available on the dates we plan to film and is very keen to work with us – he's sending a showreel, so that I can see what he's been doing more recently and to show my co-producers. Jono co-runs a company called Shooters that can provide us with the camera, grip and lighting equipment we need, as well as extra personnel such as camera assistant and grip.

Friday 21 February 2003

Fernando comes in for another costume fitting. We are going for a layered, contemporary look, based on the dancers' own street clothes, but with Fernando's skilfully selected additions from the sales.

Saturday 22 February 2003

Two weeks until the shoot and we have a long production meeting with Jo, Tracey, Kate, Karin, Sarah and myself present. We discuss the schedule, catering, heating, parking and look at Tracey and Jo's most recent cost report. So far, the only major overspend is location and heating, but we are under in other areas.

Monday 24 February 2003

Transfer footage from Friday's rehearsal into iMovie and do a rough edit. Take it in and show the dancers and Fin.

Figure 12.1 A production meeting; present were Jo Holding (Production Manager), Tracey Holder (Production co-ordinator), Karin Fisher-Potisk (co-producer), Kate Gowar (co-producer), Sarah Dowling (Production runner) and Katrina McPherson (director/co-producer)

Tuesday 25 February 2003

I'm getting nervous about having not yet confirmed a lighting cameraperson (or any equipment). But Jono's showreel arrives this morning and it looks great. I call him and book him for the job.

As he is in Italy filming, the earliest that Jono can recce the locations is Thursday 6 March, only two days before filming is scheduled to start, but he's confident that we will still be able to source everything we need in time.

Wednesday 26 February 2003

Spend the afternoon filming with Fin and the dancers in rehearsal space. The choreography looks very strong – fast, powerful, complex. The light in the studio was beautiful, which really helps me to see the potential of the filmed movement.

Figure 12.2 **In the studio, looking at material with choreographer Fin Walker (dancers Kate Gowar, Robert Tannion, Karin Fisher-Potisk and Matthew Morris)**

Fin talks about how she has the image of the four dancers being in a family-like situation, with individuals all in various relationships with each other.

Like Paulo, Fin has choreographed around 13 minutes of material. In contrast to Paulo, Fin has made many very short sequences of movement: duets, trios, quartets and solos. For each character, Fin explains, the very slow 'Way Down Deep' solo is the most personal moment – or maybe the moment of truth.

As Min is still busy on another job, we ask Sarah to take a digital stills camera round a selection of second-hand furniture stores and photograph objects that fit our design brief. Later, we sit together and make up a list of the props that we'd like for the shoot from what she has found.

Friday 28 February 2003

Fernando comes in with the final costumes. Each dancer has a number of outfits, created by mixing and matching from their individual collections. We won't know for sure if we have got the look right until we are in the locations, with lights on and looking through the camera lens.

Lighting cameraperson Jono comes in to studio to meet the dancers. He sees some of Paulo's material as the dancers are rehearsing it. They have to keep it fresh in their minds – and bodies – whilst creating with Fin. I show Jono some short excerpts of Fin's material that I have edited on my laptop.

Saturday 1 and Sunday 2 March 2003

Rest up and chill out with the family. Visit and have friends round. Feel like there is loads of preparation still to do, but also feel that it is important to have some relaxation time away from the project, before the intense two weeks ahead.

Monday 3 March 2003

Have a long meeting with Kate and Karin, during which we discuss the overall structure of the film and the role of the CCTV images. It is useful to do this now that all the dance material has been choreographed, as in effect we now know what our palette is.

I start storyboarding, in the form of lots of floor plans, showing dancers movement in relation to camera's position and movement with notes to myself on approach to filming each section. Based on this, I draft a detailed shooting schedule and e-mail it to Tracey, Kate and Karin for their input.

Wednesday 5 March 2003

Kate and Karin check over the shooting schedule. I'd forgotten a couple of short sections of Fin's, which I now include. It's going to be an extremely tight three days. Let's hope everything goes smoothly.

Thursday 6 March 2003

Recce of both interior locations with most of production team, including Jono, Min, Kate, Karin, Simon and Sarah.

Whilst at the Miro, the press officer Kathy comes in with the offer that, if we repaint the space, we can have access to film from Tuesday evening for only the extra cost of redecorating. Everyone gets very excited, as this means, in effect, gaining a whole day of filming (we were scheduled to get in on the Wednesday evening, with only a long day of filming on the Thursday).

However, before we accept this offer, we must look calmly at the overall financial implications, as this extra day will mean additional equipment and catering costs.

With this extra time and having now seen both spaces, Jono and Min all for shooting everything at Miro and forgetting about Dalston. I'm swithering, but Simon voices the concern that we will lose something if we ditch Dalston completely, i.e. a. enclosed feeling and the idea of space within spaces.

After some thought at home, I make the decision that we should go for one and a half filming days in Dalston and two days in Miro, with half a day transfer. I immediately re-do the filming schedule and realise that even with what is effectively almost an extra day, we will still be pushed to get everything filmed.

Speak to Steve at Shooters and negotiate a new price for crew and equipment for the extra day. They are being very supportive and I feel pretty confident that this side of things will come in well within budget. All the overspends so far seem to be location-related, with the latest being the unexpected, yet unavoidable cost of hiring space heaters – something that we overlooked budgeting for.

Saturday 8 March 2003

Liverpool Street Station

Day starts with everyone off to the station manager's office for a safety brief.

Set up the three DV cameras on the balcony around the station concourse. I am to operate one, with Runners Sarah and Amy on the other two. As we frame the shots, I realise with horror that since our last visit to the station a week ago, 70-centimetre-long blue 'feet' have been stuck to the white floor, making tacks across exactly the space that I had

planned to film. They are part of an advertising campaign for a telecom-
munications company. This is a disaster, as we can't just peel them off,
it would take too long to contact anyone about removing them, and we
certainly don't want them in shot.

Look to see if we can film the scenes in a different part of the station,
but no, wouldn't work. Decide that we will have to go with the feet, and
hope that framing and editing will make feet less visible.

It also becomes obvious during the day that Mat, one of the dancers, is
not well. He has been trying to put on a brave face for filming, but is
feeling very bad. We ask him to go home and rest as much as he can
before Monday, as he has four intensive days of filming ahead of him this
week.

Sunday 9 March 2003
Go to Dalston location with Kate, Karin, Simon and Jono to talk through
the material and filming plan.

Set props have been delivered to the space on the Saturday. Min and
runners Sarah and Amy are hanging wallpaper on the walls and dressing
the set.

Monday 10 March 2003

Dalston

We film everything scheduled, but the shoot feels quite chaotic. This is
a lot to do with the fact that we are a large crew in a very small space.

It is really hard only now seeing the movement in location, with props and
costumes and through the lens of the digi-beta camera, which has a
very different look to my mini-DV camera. Jono and I have to do a lot of
looking and talking to establish a shared vision. The dancers have to get
used not only to performing in these cramped spaces but also to being
surrounded by lights, a track and lots of people.

We are also dealing with the challenge of a lot of camera movement and
nowhere to hide lights or the rest of the crew. Everyone is keen to watch
the monitor, but this adds to the rather claustrophobic feeling. A couple
of times, the noise level rises (people chatting) and I'm distracted. But,
the dancers are performing wonderfully and the shots are looking great.

We wrap (end the filming day) exactly on time. I am relieved to have the first day of the full-scale shoot behind us; tomorrow, everything won't seem so new.

Mat phones me in the evening. He's still unwell and wondering if he can come in later tomorrow, as he needs extra rest to get better. I agree that he should have a late start and that we will do what we can to work round this. I am extremely worried, but we can't cancel the shoot completely, as Rob is off to Hong Kong on Friday for several months and who knows when we could all get back together again? I have to keep positive though and quickly make a new plan for tomorrow. I know that Mat will do everything he can to work through his illness.

Tuesday 11 March 2003

Dalston

When everyone is assembled at the beginning of the filming day, Simon gives a pep talk. As assistant director, he feels that he needs to remind everyone how much we need to achieve in a very short time.

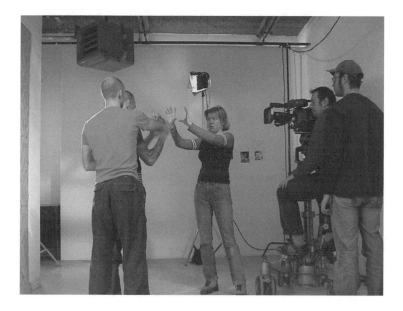

Figure 12.3 **Describing the frame to lighting cameraman (Jono Smith) and grip (Arun Taylor)**

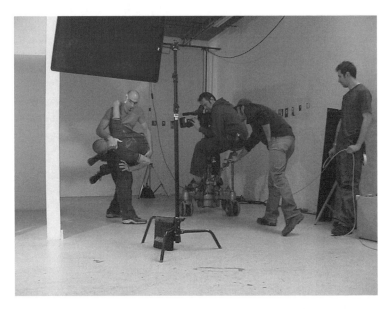

Figure 12.4 **The shot being described in Figure 12.3 is filmed**

The morning goes fine. Before we know it, we are finished at Dalston. We move to the Miro space in the afternoon and do as much setting up as we can in advance of tomorrow's shoot. Min, Amy and Sarah return to Dalston to do a proper clear-up.

Once home, I look urgently at the shooting schedule again. Mat is still unwell and we need to find a way of making it possible for him to work a shorter day tomorrow. I am beginning to have to abandon some of the planned choreography and shots.

Wednesday 12 March 2003

Miro

Really missed Fin today. Although dancers doing great with the material and Gill Clark providing excellent feedback, both to them and me, on the way that they are performing, we are a having to drop several sections of Fin's choreography, due to Mat's continued ill health. If Fin were there, she could have probably quickly reworked some of the material without Mat. Instead, all we can do is leave whole sections out.

Figure 12.5 **Filming Rob's solo; notice the boom pole with microphone attached for capturing synch sound**

Thursday 13 March 2003

Miro

Have had to drop some more of Fin's sections. I am now really worried that the overall balance will not be quite as good as planned, but what we are filming is looking amazing.

Last thing we do is to record some wild-tracks of Kate and Karin performing their solos. We do this in a small cupboard at the location, as this has the least other ambient sound. Kate and Karin do brilliantly, but say that they felt very odd breathing heavily in a broom cupboard with only a sound recordist as audience!

Saturday 15 March 2003

Travel back home. Can't believe that all the filming is complete. It is nice to have a break from the incessant logistical planning of the past month or so.

Tuesday 18 March 2003

Receive an invoice from Shooters, Jono's company. It is well under what we had budgeted for camera and lighting equipment. I am delighted and suggest immediately that we spend some of the surplus on a picture grade.

Friday 21 March 2003

First batch of transferred rushes arrive and I start to view. It's been good to have a week since the shoot before I see anything.

Monday 24 March 2003

Having looked through everything that we shot (not the station footage yet), I start logging (selecting the material that I want to take into the edit).

What do I look for? A moment that grabs me, where performance, dancers' movement, camera framing and motion come together. The lighting needs to look right. A certain energy. A shape of shot. A complexity or simplicity. An 'Ah yes' moment. I am less concerned with whole takes, more interested sections that capture the essence of a particular scene. The footage is looking great.

Monday 31 March 2003

Simon and I sit down in the edit together. Simon has already tried out some sketches of ideas for some of the sections.

We look through all the material again. We select more definite in and out points, looking carefully at each section and discussing what it is we like about individual moments. Material is continually discarded – this is a constant process of stripping down.

Saturday 5 April 2003

Send off VHS tapes with our first edit to Kate and Karin and composer Ben.

Saturday 12 April 2003

Receive feedback (via e-mail) from Kate and Karin. Their main comments are about the length of a few of the sections (some feel too long, a couple feel too short), a few moments that they know were filmed and that are now missing (there's quite a lot of material 'on the edit suite floor', but Kate and Karin only question a couple) and the overall structure.

Monday 21 April 2003

Restart off-line edit.

Simon and I look through the selection I have made from the CCTV footage. We have shot each 'dramatic interaction' with three cameras, each offering a different perspective on the action.

Looking for the right way to use these images. Also concerned that the viewer will not necessarily easily pick out who amongst the many people passing through shot are our characters. Look at digitally zooming into the images, thus focusing the shot on our characters and their moments of interaction.

The digital zoom also degrades the images, which adds to the CCTV effect, but Simon is not going to spend too much time on creating exactly the image quality (in terms of colour and quality) as this will all have to be redone in the on-line.

Tuesday 22 and Wednesday 23 April 2003

Spend another couple of days editing the dance sections.

Realise that with the material as it is now, the film will run to around 28 minutes. I worry that it might be too long – Will people ever choose to sit down and watch a half-hour dance film at a festival? Kate and Karin say that they would be delighted to have a half-hour video dance, as it would be good as part of a double bill with a live work, which is how they plan to tour next year.

Watch a VHS that Ben has sent up with some of his music laid onto our off-line edit. Catch glimpses of the music taking the atmosphere of the work onto a whole new level. Exciting! My only concern is that it is quite heavy on percussion and how that will work with the rhythms of the synch sound also audible in the mix.

Having e-mail discussions with Kate and Karin about the title. No one happy with *In Truth* – it feels clumsy, especially when you write – or say, 'In *In Truth*'. Another option, *Double Take*, feels cinematic, but Karin and Kate would like to make reference to that fact that the starting point for both choreographers was an exploration of the 'truth'.

Thursday 15 and Friday 16 May 2003

Kate and Karin come up to the Highlands to spend a couple of days finalising the off-line. Together, we agree on some adjustments to the order of the different sections.

Had feedback from the choreographers. Paulo really happy; Fin concerned that the use of synch sound in the off-line makes her choreography seem quite harsh. We agree that Ben's music will help to bring out the more subtle energies in her movement.

We also watch and listen to the latest VHS that Ben has sent us with his composed music. In general, we feel it could be more daring (sometimes it feels too much like 'background music'), more varied and that there is possibly too much of it – the impact of the music would be increased if it wasn't running throughout the video dance. I make plenty of notes which I'll feed back to Ben.

We need to make a final decision about the title. Through discussion, we realise that 'Double Take' is what the video dance does, whereas 'The Truth' is what it is about, so we go with the latter. Feels like the right decision and Karin says that her solar plexus no longer feels tight!

Saturday 17 May 2003

Simon prepares material for the on-line edit, which he will also do, but on a higher-spec edit system than the one we used for the off-line.

Tracey and I start to gather names for the credits, compiling a list via e-mail.

Monday 19, Tuesday 20 and Wednesday 21 May 2003

On-line edit in Edinburgh where we add titles and credits. It's amazing to see the work at such a high quality.

I speak to Ben on the phone about the music. The conclusion is that he needs a bit more time, so I but back the dub by another couple of days. It will be tight for the premiere on 12 June, but hopefully we won't run up against any problems.

Tuesday 27 May 2003

Today is the picture grading. Katherine Grincell at Blue is a superb colourist. In her hands, the video dance takes on a whole new feel, as she corrects and balances the colours, taking away green tones, enhancing the tones, making the whites whiter and the blacks deeper. It's the final polish that makes *The Truth* vibrant and lush – perfect for the big screen.

Wednesday 28 May 2003

Yesterday's grade was the final bit of work to be done on the visual side of things (apart from the design of the tape and DVD boxes and publicity material). It is now time to focus 100 per cent on the soundtrack.

I spend a couple of days with Ben in his sound studio. Together, we look at making sections of the music simpler and adding new sounds and textures to others.

Monday 2 June and Tuesday 3 June 2003

Ben sends music up by courier overnight. There is some problem with the computer files and we lose several hours of dub time.

By lunchtime Tuesday, it's clear that we are not going to get finished. Neither John Cobban, the dubbing mixer, nor I want to rush the final mix down of the soundtrack, so we arrange that I will come back in on Sunday. If all goes to plan, this will leave three days for safety copies to be made before the premiere screening on the Thursday.

Sunday 8 June 2003

Final day of dub. John has added incorporated synch sounds and actuality into the soundtrack. The music is very powerful, but sometimes it feels like there is not enough space for the sound of the dancers moving and breathing, which I think are also essential.

In the end, I think we achieve the balance – John does two versions of the final mix down – one for television and monitors, the other for projection.

Thursday 12 June 2003

Kate, Karin and Jo fly up for the world premiere of *The Truth* at Dundee Contemporary Arts, Scotland.

We had decided to make an evening's programme by first screening *Pace*, *Moment* and *Sense-8*, short video dance works that I have directed, and Simon has edited. This first half of the programme provides a context for *The Truth* and 'warms up' the audience.

It is both nerve-wracking and spell-binding to see and hear *The Truth*, fully dubbed and graded and projected off a pristine new screening copy. The sound works marvellously through the cinema speakers and the images look bold up there on the big screen.

At the reception afterwards, Kate, Karin and I answer questions from the audience. Most people seem really impressed. Plenty love the soundtrack. None of the questions asked are ones that we could have anticipated; all throw new light on this brand new video dance, and I realise that, already at this first screening, *The Truth* has left home and is forging its own way in the world.

Glossary

actuality sound Any sound that is generated by the dancers or other animate figure or object, on screen.

aperture The opening at the back of a lens that allows light into the lens. The size of the aperture – and therefore how much light is allowed in – is controlled by the iris.

auto Refers to when the camera, rather than the operator, has control of a feature, such as auto-focus or auto-exposure. If possible, it is best to over-ride the auto functions and operate everything manually, as this will give you more control over the aesthetic of your work.

birds eye A camera position that places the camera above the action.

boom A long pole onto which a microphone is attached.

budget The amount of money available for your project and how it is to be spent.

cable basher A person on the shoot who makes sure that any cables do not get caught up in the track or trip anyone up.

camera operator A skilled person who is responsible for the framing and movement of each shot.

camera re-work Making a video dance based on an already existing live choreography that has (usually) had a life in the theatre.

capture The process of filmed images being taken into a digital editing system.

choreography The composition of repeatable movement.

clip A section of filmed material in the edit.

continuity An approach to filming in which shots and editing create the illusion that the sequence of movement on screen has the same linear structure as it had in live performance. **Continuity** is also the term used to describe the need for the on-screen detail, such as direction of travel or costume, to remain consistent between shots if the illusion of continuity is to achieved.

copyright   Indicates who has ownership of the completed video dance, in terms of having the right to produce and distribute copies of the work and to give consent to screenings and broadcast.

costume   What the performers are wearing on-screen.

collaboration   Two or more people working together on a project.

commission   The process of giving money for a particular project, usually for a specific series or scheme.

composer   Someone who writes original music for the screen.

cut   The immediate and complete transition from one clip to the next. The 'cut' can also mean the overall structure of the edited work.

design   Attention to the colour, shape and texture of everything that comes into frame.

diffuse light   A soft, even and widespread quality of light.

digital video   Electronically recorded moving images and sound designed to be seen and heard via a screen.

director   The person who is ultimately responsible for the overall work.

director of photography   An experienced cameraperson who is responsible for the overall look of a film in terms of how it is lit and shot.

dissolve   In editing, when one clip is gradually replaced by another.

dubbing mixer   A skilled individual who creates the final soundtrack, by placing and mixing all the different audio elements onto the master tape.

executive producer   An individual representing a broadcaster or funding body who has responsibility for overseeing a production.

exposure   The allowing of light into the lens, via the aperture, thereby creating a film or video image.

focus   An in-focus image is crisp and clearly defined, whereas an out-of-focus image is blurred. Whilst having images in focus is the norm, having some or all of a frame out of focus can be a skilful way of guiding the viewer's eye or creating an evocative effect.

focus puller   An assistant cameraperson whose responsibilities include controlling the focus of a shot.

format   Refers to the type of tape or disk that material is recorded onto, as defined by its size and by the quality at which the images and sound will be encoded. Different formats include DV Cam, Digital Beta, VHS, etc.

frame   The rectangular image seen through a lens. Frame is also the term given to the individual images that make up a film or video picture and which are referenced by time-code, for example, there are twenty-five or twenty-nine frames per second of shot video.

gaffer   See 'spark'

grip   Specialist equipment that is used to support and move the camera. The person who operates this equipment is also called the grip.

handheld   Operating a camera whilst holding it in your hands.

in point   The starting point of a new clip in an edited sequence.

improvisation   Creating material by making decisions as you go, usually based on a 'score', i.e. a set of rules or restrictions.

iris   The device at the back of the lens, created by a series of thin metal plates and forming an expandable circle, which controls how much light enters the aperture. The camera's iris functions much like the iris of an eye.

lamp   A specialist film or video light.

lighting camera   Skilled person who both lights the location and operates the camera.

location   The place, interior or exterior, in which filming takes place.

location scout   Person who searches for suitable places in which to film.

logging   The process of selecting what of your filmed material will be taken into the edit.

master tape   The name given to the tape onto which the final version of your video dance is output from the edit system. It is from this tape that all copies of the work will be made.

monitor   A television screen on which to watch the output of the camera, or in the edit suite.

montage   An approach to filming and editing in which shots from different time and space contexts are put together to create an order that is unique to the screen.

narrative   The structure resulting from the telling of a story.

non-linear   Not following in a sequential order. Non-linear editing usually refers to digital systems where the order of images can easily be altered.

out-point   The end of a new clip in an edited sequence.

off-line   The stage in the post-production process during which creative decisions are made about the overall shape of the video dance and the order in which the shots are placed.

on-line   The stage in the post-production process during which the technical aspects of the final work are worked on and, usually, titles and on-screen graphics are added.

picture grade   A post-production procedure which involves correcting and altering the colour of each individual on-screen image.

pitch   A meeting in which you describe your project to a potential funder with the purpose of trying to encourage them to give you the money.

post-production   All the work that happens after the shoot until the video dance is complete.

pre-production   All the preparatory work that takes place before a shoot.

production designer   Responsible for the look of everything that appears in shot.

production manager   Co-ordinates the production and looks after paperwork.

producer   The member of the team who is primarily responsible for the financial and organisational aspects of a production, working closely with the director.

prop   Short for property: any object used or seen on screen.

recce   A visit to a prospective filming location with the purpose of finding out its suitability for filming.

shooting schedule   A document detailing the plans for a day of filming.

shot list   A list of all the material that you hope to film. It is sometimes useful to order according to priority.

storyboard   A series of drawn images representing how you plan to film, and edit, your video dance.

soundtrack   The aural accompaniment to your video dance work.

soundtrack designer   Someone who creates the soundtrack of the video dance.

spark   A film or video lighting professional. Also known as a gaffer.

synch sound   The short term for 'synchronised sound', which refers to the situation in which an image and any sound that it makes are simultaneously recorded onto the video tape.

theme   A single idea to which all aspects of the work relate.

title-safe   The area on screen on which any graphics or text will be seen on most televisions, monitors or projection screens.

time-code   As the pictures and sound is recorded onto the tape in the camera, each frame is given a unique time-code number.

track   Lightweight metal rails, like train tracks, used to move the camera smoothly across the floor.

treatment   A written description of what the finished video dance will be like. Used as a selling document and to clarify a vision between collaborators.

tripod   A three-legged structure designed to support the camera.

viewfinder   The part of the camera that you look through to see what the lens is framing.

white balance   A system by which the video camera reproduces colour, using white as the base line. As the quality of white changes according to the light it is under, the white balance setting within the camera must also be altered, in order to give a true representation of the various colours.

wildtrack   Actuality sound recorded separately from any visual images.

video dance   An art form that fuses avant-garde approaches to dance-making with innovation in video art, film and television-making practices.

Contributors

Liz Aggiss and **Billy Cowie** are Brighton-based artists, collaborating and touring the UK and Europe since 1980. Their screen dance work includes *Beethoven in Love* and *Motion Control*, both made for the BBC/Arts Council England Dance for the Camera series; *Anarchic Variations*, commissioned as part of by the Arts Council England's Capture series; and *Break*, for Channel 4. Liz Aggiss is Professor of Visual Performance at the University of Brighton where Billy Cowie is a Principal Research Fellow. Their book *Anarchic Dance* is published by Routledge.

Lea Anderson is a choreographer and founder member for the all-female The Cholmondeleys dance company. She has created many live and screen works for The Cholmondeleys and their brother company The Featherstonehaughs. Her screen choreography credits include *Cross Channel* (BBC), *Perfect Moment* and *Waiting* (both Channel 4), which she also directed. She made *Speed Ramp* for the Arts Council of England's Capture series, co-directed *The Featherstonehaughs Draw on the Sketchbooks of Egon Schiele* (BBC) and has directed a camera re-work of *Double Take*.

Litza Bixler was born in the USA, now lives in the UK and works all over the world. She trained as a director, dancer and photographer, and has a MA in Choreography. In addition to making video dance, she also choreographs promos, adverts and feature films. Litza is one half of the directing/production duo Dust Baby, which she set up with Deveril in 2000 and whose credits include *Heart Thief* for Channel 4's 4Dance series, in which she also performed.

Erin Brannigan is the director of ReelDance International Dance on Screen Festival in Australia, and has curated dance screen programmes for Melbourne International Arts Festival 2003 and other international dance screen festivals. She writes about dance for newspapers and completed her PhD thesis on 'A Cinema of Movement: Dance and the Moving Image'.

Elliot Caplan was filmmaker-in-residence at the Cunningham Dance Foundation from 1983 to 1998, collaborating with Merce Cunningham and John Cage in the production of many award-winning films and videos including, *Beach Birds for Camera* and *Points in Space*. Caplan's more recent films have been produced through his New York-based company, Picture Start Films and include *UTango*, *Steelworks*, made with choreographer Robert Poole, and *Close-Up on Berlin* commissioned by the Deutsche Tanzfilm Institute.

John Cobban is a much sought-after composer and dubbing mixer who has worked on countless short films, documentaries and feature films. He created the soundtracks for Katrina McPherson's video dance works *Swoop*, *Sense-8*, *There's Something You Should Know* and the award-winning *Moment*. He was also dubbing mixer on *The Truth*.

Billy Cowie (see **Liz Aggiss**).

Simon Fildes is an visual artist and editor who has made many video art works that have been shown at festivals across Europe. Simon has edited many broadcast programmes, as well as most of the video dance works directed by his partner Katrina McPherson, including *Pace*, *Sense-8*, *Moment* and *The Truth*. Recently, Katrina and Simon have been collaborating on dance works for the web, including www.hyperchoreography.org and the video dance portal www.video dance.org.uk.

Karin Fisher-Potisk founded Ricochet Dance Company with Kate Gowar and as joint artistic director and dancer with the company, she has commissioned and performed in over thirty new works. Karin performed in Peter Greenaway's dance film for television *M is for Man, Music, Mozart*, and she was a dancer in *The Truth*, directed by Katrina McPherson, which Ricochet commissioned and co-produced.

David Hinton is an award-winning British director best known for his screen versions of stage shows by DV8 Physical Theatre: *Dead Dreams of Monochrome Men* and *Strange Fish*. He has also made films with the Alvin Ailey Company, Adventures in Motion Pictures and the Royal Swedish Ballet, and has collaborated with choreographers Wendy Houstoun, Russell Maliphant and Rosemary Lee to create original dance works for the screen.

Neville Kidd films high-quality documentaries and factual series for the BBC and Channel 4, as well as dramas and feature films for broadcast and cinema. He and Katrina McPherson have often worked together on documentaries and he was lighting cameraman on her video dance works, *Moment* and *Sense-8*.

Rosemary Lee has worked extensively with film and video, closely collaborating with a range of artist/filmmakers (Peter Anderson, Nic Sandiland and David Hinton). These projects have included live performance merging with video projection, installations, documentary and four short dance films commissioned for television: *boy*, *greenman*, *Infanta* and *Snow*.

Bob Lockyer has spent the past forty years directing and producing dance for television and regularly teaches workshops all over the world. Bob was responsible, with Rodney Wilson, for setting up BBC Television's successful Dance for the Camera series, a format that has been copied internationally.

Ross MacGibbon was a dancer in the Royal Ballet in England before becoming a photographer, editor and then director of dance films. He collaborated with choreographer Yolande Snaith to make *Should Accidentally Fall* and with Mark Baldwin to make *Echo* for BBC's

Dance for the Camera series, and he is responsible for the television versions of many large-scale ballet productions.

Miranda Melville has designed extensively for theatre, opera, film and dance. Her work for dance film includes *Cross Channel*, choreographed by Lea Anderson and directed by Margaret Williams; *Outside In*, with Candoco Dance Company; *Fresh Dances*, choreographed by Matthew Hawkins and directed by Deborah May; and *Where Angels Fear to Tread*, choreographed and directed by Mark Murphy. Miranda was the production designer on *The Truth*.

Laura Taler is a Romanian born choreographer/director who lives and works in Canada. Her award-winning dance films, which include *The Village Trilogy*, *Heartland*, *Dances for a Small Screen* and *Death and the Maiden*, have been broadcast on television in Canada, the USA, the UK, Australia and the Netherlands as well as at numerous festivals and special screenings across the world.

More information about the work of all the above contributors and links to related web sites can be found at www.makingvideodance.com

Resources

This is a list of published books about dance on screen.

Dodds, S. (2001) *Dance on Screen: genres and media from Hollywood to experimental art*, Basingstoke: Palgrave.

Jordan, S. and D. Allen (eds) (1993) *Parallel Lines: Media Representations of Dance*, London: John Libbey & Company Ltd.

Mitoma, J. (ed.) (2002) *Envisioning Dance on Film and Video*, London and New York: Routledge.

www.videodance.org.uk
A web site providing information related to making, promoting and viewing dance on the screen.

www.makingvideodance.com has additional, up-to-date resources as well as links to other useful web sites. You can also buy DVDs of Katrina McPherson's video-dance work on this site.

Index

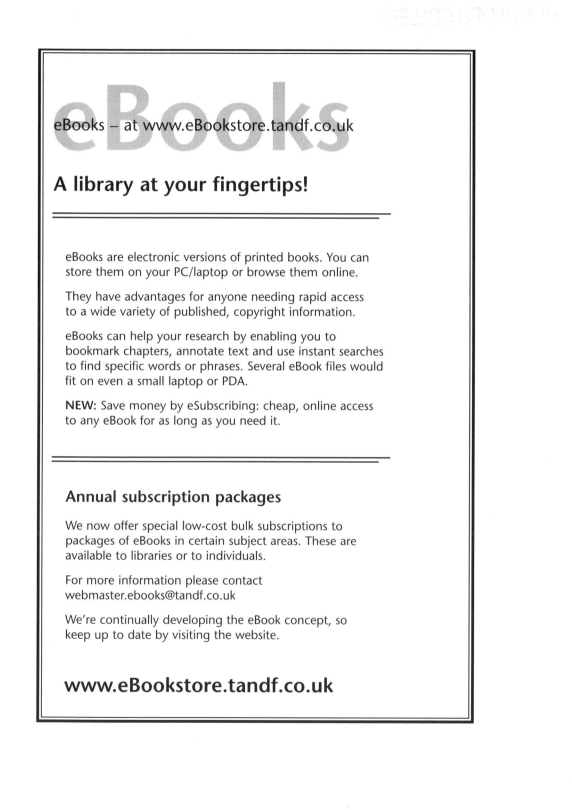

7 DAY
BOOK

GUILDFORD **college**

Learning Resource Centre

Please return on or before the last date shown.
No further issues or renewals if any items are overdue.

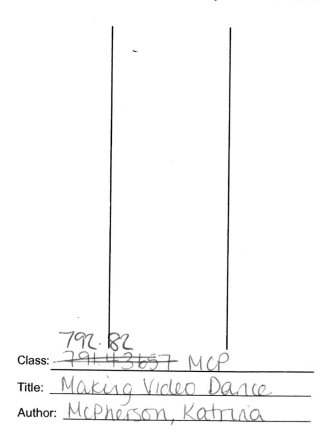

Class: 792.82 ~~791.43657~~ MCP

Title: Making Video Dance

Author: McPherson, Katrina